JEAN MARLOW

AUDITION SPEECHES
for WOMEN

Routledge • New York

To
BRIAN SCHWARTZ
'Thank you'

First published in the USA and Canada in 2001
by Theatre Arts Books / Routledge
29 West 35 Street, New York NY 10001
www.routledge-ny.com

© 2001 Jean Marlow

ISBN 0-87830-146-1

CIP catalogue record available at the Library of Congress.

Originally published in 2001
by A & C Black (Publishers) Limited
37 Soho Square, London W1D 3QZ

All rights reserved. No part of this publication may be
reproduced in any form or by any means — graphic,
electronic or mechanical, including photocopying, recording, taping or information storage and retrieval systems —
without the written permission of the publisher

Typeset by Florence Production Ltd in 10 on12 pt Garamond Book
Printed and bound in Great Britain by Creative Print
and Design (Wales), Ebbw Vale

JEAN MARLOW

Is it really five years since her first books of audition speeches, *Actors'/Actresses' Audition Speeches – for All Ages and Accents* were published? Well the moving finger writes and relentlessly moves on. In these last five years the theatre has kept alive and kicking and Jean has managed to keep her finger on the pulse of a very unpredictable patient. Perhaps one of the most welcome aspects of her work in compiling this latest collection, is her awareness of the nerve jangling process of auditioning for work in a highly competitive profession – and I applaud the success she has had in finding colleagues to give their excellent advice on auditioning and developing new skills to open up more casting opportunities. As well as her invaluable input as co-director of The Actors' Theatre School, she has in the interim played in *The Importance of Being Earnest, Romeo and Juliet* and toured in *Pride and Prejudice* in the theatre, worked in films and television and completed another six audition books.

Her latest collection of up-to-the-minute speeches should prove invaluable to the actor seeking new audition material. I wish you every success.

Eamonn Jones
The Actors' Theatre School

CONTENTS

AUDITION SPEECHES

ACKNOWLEDGEMENTS

I would like to say thank you to the actors, directors, playwrights, casting directors, agents and publishers who have kindly contributed to this book.

In particular I would mention Athos Antoniades, Corinne Beaver, Tay Brandon, Frances Cuka, Kevin Daly, April De Angelis, Ellen Dryden, Gillian Diamond, Sue Gibbons, Alison Gorton, John Higgins, James Hogan, Rona Laurie, Jacky Matthews, Katie Mitchell, Hannah Newman, John Quinlan (IT support), Keith Salberg, Carol Schroder, Don Taylor, Drew Rhys Williams. Also Brian Schwartz and Offstage Bookshop, and my editors, Tesni Hollands and Katie Taylor. And not forgetting my co-director, Eamonn Jones of The Actors' Theatre School, and the students themselves who tried out all these speeches for me.

PREFACE

The new millennium has brought some big surprises, not least of all in the world of entertainment where boundaries have been stretched often to unbelievable limits. The 'New Writing Seasons' have thrown up new challenges in theatre, films, television and radio – as have the latest versions, adaptations and revivals of old classics. And every day, more and more is being demanded of actors.

The Peter Hall Company's highly acclaimed production of John Barton's *Tantalus* opened at the Denver Center for the Performing Arts in Denver, Colorado in October 2000. It runs from ten o'clock in the morning until half past ten at night, with intervals, and is described as 'an epic theatre myth for the millennium'. In a cast of twenty-seven British and American actors, and with the use of masks, the eight leading performers play a wide variety of parts throughout this ten hour marathon.

Over here, the Royal National Theatre presented *House and Garden* – two plays performed simultaneously by the same cast in two adjacent auditoria. Yes, you have to be fit to work in the theatre today!

Most of the extracts used in these two new books – one for Men and one for Women – are from recent productions, some of them still running in London at the time of writing. Alan Ayckbourn's very funny *Comic Potential* with its look into the near future of TV soaps when actors have finally been replaced by 'actoids', David Hare's disturbing *Murmuring Judges* and Richard Norton-Taylor's *The Colour of Justice*, documenting the controversial Stephen Lawrence trial, all reflect the age we live in and are among many of the up-to-the-minute plays used here. I have also included extracts from film scripts such as *Pulp Fiction* and Mike Leigh's *Life is Sweet*.

All the speeches have been tried and tested by students from The Actors' Theatre School, either in workshops, at auditions, or in the London Academy of Music and Dramatic Art (LAMDA) and Guildhall School of Music and Drama examinations. As far as possible I have avoided using extracts included in other audition books.

I hope these books will fulfil a need for both student and professional actors alike, and also be a reminder of the many good plays seen in London and the provinces – and often too briefly on the 'fringe'.

MORE ABOUT AUDITIONING

You've made up your mind to become an actor. But before you can even begin you're faced with 'competition'. You apply for drama school, but first you have to be selected from what seems like hundreds of other people who all have the same idea. You have to audition. 'Fear of failure' starts to creep up on you. And you have to push it away, otherwise it can 'dog' you all the way through your life as an actor. An audition or 'casting' is not an examination or some sort of test to see who gets the highest grades. It may not seem fair at the time, but very often you just weren't what the auditioner, director or casting director was looking for. You didn't fit the bill.

A friend of mine, not long out of drama school, was touring in a production of *Spring and Port Wine* playing 'Hilda', the daughter of a strict father who is determined to make her eat a herring for dinner which she hates. Throughout the play the herring is put before Hilda at every meal, but she steadfastly refuses to eat it. Then the herring disappears and the family cat is suspected. The cat was played by a large ginger tom called Hughie – that only his owner could love. The show went well, the notices were good, and when a casting director came in on the second week of the tour, the actors had high hopes of getting 'something on television'. To everyone's astonishment the only actor offered a part was Hughie. The casting director was casting a cat food commercial. Suddenly Hughie had become a star and the film company sent a limousine to take him to the studios each day.

Always remember you haven't failed. You simply weren't selected – and in this case the cat got the job!

A musical director, who has sat through hundreds of auditions for West End musicals confirmed this. If someone arrives to audition and they are not what the director has in mind, they will probably be stopped after a few bars of music and sent away with a 'Thank you, we'll let you know.' The next artist to arrive may not be nearly as good, but will often get a recall because he or she looks right for the part.

A director is just as anxious to cast the right person as you are to get the job, particularly if he is putting on a whole season of plays. Does this actor look young enough to play down to seventeen, can this actress age from twenty to forty-five. Are they going to contrast well with the rest of the company who have already been cast? Should we be looking for a 'name'? It is not always the best actor or actress that gets the part. How can it be?

So throw 'failure' and 'rejection' out of your vocabulary. As long as you've done your very best to prepare for your audition, you haven't failed, you've simply added to your experience and may even be called back another time. Only the other day an actor telephoned to say he had just auditioned for a lead in the tour of *Joseph and the Amazing Technicolor Dreamcoat*. The director told him he was wrong for the part, but liked his audition and arranged to see him again for a new show being cast at the end of the month.

But let's have a look at the first audition you are most likely to encounter when you are thinking about 'going into the business' – the drama school audition.

The Drama School Audition

Tim Reynolds, Principal of the Academy Drama School, White-chapel, has this advice for would be drama students:

'I pondered for some time, wondering what could possibly be added to the advice already given in Jean's earlier books, *Actors'/Actresses' Audition Speeches – for All Ages and Accents*. Then I decided simply to put in writing the advice and help we give to those students who are on our one year Medallion Course – for seventeen to twenty year olds – which is solely dedicated to preparing them to audition for drama school, and for the reality of the three-year course they are hoping to enter.

First. Be very sure of your dedication. Drama schools are not about getting into television soap operas, or block-busting movies. They are more concerned with training your talents to the extent that you can rise to any challenge that may come your way. Although some actors achieve fame and fortune, most do not, and unless you feel sure that working regularly in the profession you love is sufficient reward, think again before you embark on a training you will probably never complete.

Do not undertake to audition for drama school until you feel entirely prepared. Although it is true to say that the people who are auditioning you want to offer you a place, there is enormous competition from other applicants. If you come to your audition with a clear understanding of your speeches and a strong idea of what you want to do with them, that's half the battle. The Academy audition literally hundreds of prospective students each year, so we have a very good idea of what we are looking for. Here are a few tips which may be of help.

Audition for all the drama schools, even the ones that are not on the top of your list. The more auditions you attend the better you get at auditioning and the better your chances. If you decide that there is only one school you could possibly go to, and then don't get in you'll have to wait 'till next year to apply again, and this could go on until you collect your pension. Strike while the iron is hot, and increase your chances. You may get more than one offer, so you could have a choice. If you do, it's important that you go to the one in which you felt most comfortable at your audition.

Find out as much as you can about the school for which you are auditioning. Each school has its own criteria, and to an extent, its own method of training, and it is as well to know as much about that particular school as possible. For example, the Academy is most widely known for being the first full time evening and weekend drama school, training over six terms which are on average twelve weeks in length. This kind of information is available in the various prospectuses, which you should study with great care before your audition.

Look very carefully at the requirements for the audition, and make sure you follow them to the letter. There may well be a workshop. Listen carefully to the instructions given, and if there is anything you do not understand, you must ask. Always be in good time for your audition. Punctuality is essential in the acting business, and this must start with your training. Know your speeches thoroughly. Not just well enough to recall the lines, but so well that you can concentrate entirely on the character you are playing. You are likely to be asked to do the speech in an entirely different way, and time and again I have seen prospective students totally unable to recall the speech under such conditions.

The speeches from this book are chosen with care, but they are only a section of the play. What has your character done or lived through before the speech begins? What will he or she go on to do afterwards. It is vital that you read the whole play, not just because you will be asked questions on it, though you well might, but you yourself will have become familiar with the person you are playing. Every character must start with you, so it is important that you pick someone that you understand, who in other circumstances could be you. Do not choose a character too old, or too young, or whose experience of life is vastly different from yours. The auditioners only need a few lines to know whether you are right for them.

Should you get help with your speeches? Well, yes, I think you should, although some drama schools advise against it. They have seen all too many times the young hopeful before them spouting lines and carefully rehearsed gestures that have been drilled into them by someone whom the procession has passed by, and who would like to live again through you. The right tuition is important. The auditioners want to see your performance and a good tutor will help you realise your performance, rather than give you theirs.

There are one or two drama schools who supply a list of speeches from which to choose. It is not a good idea to do these speeches for other auditions because they are known to the other schools and it might appear that you are simply too lazy to learn another speech.

Finally, it is important to realize that the odds against you getting into any particular drama school of necessity are high, as they are when you have completed your training. The advice you are being given at the beginning of this book should be used to shorten those odds. At the end of the day, though, when you are turned down, remember it is only the decision of that particular school, and only at that particular time. Never lose confidence in yourself or your abilities.

The best of luck. If you've got the will, the heart and the stamina, combined of course with the talent, you'll get there.'

Robert Palmer, is Senior Voice Tutor at the Royal Academy of Dramatic Art (RADA) which auditions between 1400 and 1500 students a year for 30 available places. He had this to say about the importance of a clear, audible voice:

'After auditioning for a place at the Royal Academy of Dramatic Art, workshops are held to determine further the technical and interpretive ability of selected candidates, particularly in a class situation.

On this occasion the Voice Department teachers give an individual ear-test where the candidate is required to sing/hum different notes played for them on the piano, sing a song and give a 'cold' reading of a text, also to participate in voice and speech exercises with a class.

During this the teacher is noting details of the actor's voice-quality, vocal range and speech, in particular any specific voice problems.

As these auditions draw in people from all over the world, the expectation has to be, as in any audition, that the actor is clearly audible and distinct – whatever their own particular dialect or accent.

Therefore it is essential that prior to the event the importance of maintaining a good standard of spoken delivery is realised. It is suggested that the regular practice of voice and speech exercises involving breath-support, resonance and articulation are necessary to underpin both classical and modern material used in the audition.'

Working Today in Professional Theatre

Sir Peter Hall created the Royal Shakespeare Company (which he ran from 1960-68) and directed the National Theatre from 1973-88. During that time he opened its new premises on the South Bank. After his repertory season at the Old Vic, he ran the Peter Hall Company in the West End until 1999 and has since opened his highly praised production of John Barton's *Tantalus* at the Denver Center for the Performing Arts in Denver, Colorado – transferring it to the Barbican Theatre, London in 2001. He has this to say about creative work in the theatre:

'Creative work in a theatre has always been done by a company. Here is another paradox. A company does the best work – but good work can also create a company. It may form itself by chance because a collection of actors in a commercial production have worked together in the past. Or it may be stimulated by the playwright's demands or the director's inspiration. It can happen in a matter of days. But the potent theatre company takes longer to develop, as actors grow together, learning each other's working habits, learning indeed how they dislike as much as how they like each other. Making theatre needs everyone to accept that they are dependent on everyone else. The messenger with one line can ruin the leading actor's scene if he does not speak at the right tempo and in the right mood. The wig-mistress who is late for a quick change can wreck the concentration of everyone on stage. Company work recognises dependency. Indeed it celebrates it . . . At the Old Vic with our small company of actors we found that the audiences' traditional responses were still strong: they loved seeing the same actors in different parts; they had an enthusiasm for seeing young talent develop; a feeling that the group had a strong and intimate relationship with it which was growing with every production. The more cohesive the company became, the more it felt capable of an immediate dialogue with its audience, and the more it felt able to arouse an imaginative response. This is the true process of live theatre.'

Developing Extra Skills

More and more demands are being made upon actors today. In the *Equity Job Information News* recently, actors and actresses were wanted for the excellent London Bubble Theatre's production of *Sleeping Beauty*. They had to be able to sing, play a musical instrument and jive. Without these extra skills, however good a performer you might be, there is no sense in even applying for an audition like this.

Jacqueline Leggo, Agent and Personal Manager, submits artistes for theatre, film, television and radio and has clients working, at the time of writing, with the Royal Shakespeare Company, the touring musical of *One Step Beyond*, the West End musical of *Buddy* and television series such as *Nuts and Bolts* (HTV) and *Without Motive* (ITV). She has this to say:

'When arranging interviews it is important to know that the performer is well equipped with contrasting audition speeches. It would be wonderful if we were always given enough time to prepare pieces which could be angled towards a particular job, but quite often an interview will be for the next day. If an artiste has a repertoire of speeches then the likelihood is that one of the pieces will be suitable. It is important to realise there is a great deal of competition for the available jobs and these days, with many musicals providing work, having one or two songs prepared as well, can only help open up opportunities. Any additional skills are certainly worth mentioning on your CV. For example playing a musical instrument, languages, fencing, horse riding – football has been asked for most recently for *Dream Team* – and driving a car is always a useful asset.'

Jean Hornbuckle trained with the Royal Academy of Music. She is an opera and recital singer and coaches singers and actors for musicals:

'Actors are often requested to prepare a song – sometimes a particular style is specified, or it can be a free choice. Many find this daunting and doubt their singing is good enough, although with the help of a teacher, it is probable that they could acquit themselves perfectly adequately.

Musical ability of any sort is a definite advantage as it can open up opportunities for actors in more varied fields, particularly in musicals where small parts involve only a little singing.

Recently, a well known writer on musical affairs wrote an article bemoaning the dreadful standard of singing in West End shows at the moment, and asking where the good singers in this country are. It cannot be denied there is a real need for well trained singers to meet composers' requirements.

A good understanding of the singing voice and a secure technique are absolutely essential for sustaining a career in any type of music from pop and jazz through to serious classical, and only with proper training can the vocal stamina required to sustain a long run in a show be built up.

Prolonged misuse of the singing voice through ignorance of these things can lead to serious vocal problems affecting both singing and speaking voice, and it is worth considering having singing lessons both to learn about correct use of the voice, and also gain confidence to present a song successfully at an audition.'

Barry Grantham, author of *Playing Commedia*, performer, director and teacher specialising in Commedia dell'Arte and other forms of physical theatre, is also well aware of the additional skills expected of actors today:

'There was a time when all you needed was a small selection of modern and classical audition pieces, a good voice (with a 'Queen's English' accent of course), a few funny dialects, and, perhaps even more important than any of these, a good wardrobe; later you might need some talent but at least you knew where to start. Now you don't know where you are – there is a chance for a part in a prestigious production of *Timon of Athens*, but your agent tells you that you must be able to play the saxaphone and drive a motorbike through a burning hoop. You know the *'Mercy'* speech from *Merchant of Venice* but can you act it while juggling five balls?

You cannot be ready for every quirky possibility but you can prepare for some of the things most likely to be demanded of you by today's theatre, where the straight play is a rarity rather than the norm (much of the repertoire of our National Theatre is devoted to musicals and other 'Total Theatre' productions).

First, perhaps, there is a much greater need to equip yourself by training in movement of all kinds: dancing, mime, stage fighting, acrobatics, period dance and styles, movement which indicates status, comedy and eccentric behaviour. It is a good idea too to treat seriously any time spent on preparation for a musical you may be involved in. You may never be or wish to be in a musical but the experience of its multiple demands will be invaluable. Masks are now often called for and there is a very specialized technique required for working in the different types of mask from the epic full masks of Greek theatre to the half-masks of Commedia dell'Arte. Then there is the whole area of improvisation, which in present training tends to concentrate on soul searching, character analysis on the Stanislavsky model – valuable but not of much help in the 'instant impro' so frequently part of today's audition process.

Perhaps surprisingly, if we look for an all embracing technique to provide us with a training that will fit us for these most recent requirements we cannot do better than to call upon that most ancient of disciplines, the Commedia dell'Arte – or more exactly *Commedia* – the shortened version now used to denote all the skills, but not necessarily involving the historic characters of Arlecchino, Colombina, Pantalone and so on. Here we have physical theatre at its most intense. Here is mask work, mime, movement, comedy, timing, audience communication, and instantaneous improvisation. It can incorporate any performing skill: dance, acrobatics, vocal and instrumental music, circus skills, all fitted into a dramatic framework that can be as truthful as anything demanded by the most dedicated followers of the Method (though its affinities are perhaps closer to Brecht and Grotowski). Unfortunately most drama schools give only a peripheral glimpse of Commedia at best, but gradually it is becoming evident that it should form a central element of any actor's training, sharing equal time with that devoted to Shakespeare, the modern masters, and the training approaches of both the Method style and traditional tuition.'

Penny Dyer, dialect coach for *The Blue Room* with Nicole Kidman and Ian Glenn at the Donmar Warehouse and on Broadway, and the film *Elizabeth* with Cate Blanchett and Geoffrey Rush:

'Never use an accent for the accent's sake. It doesn't impress. Only use what is relevant to the character and the rhythms of the writing. Make sure you feel comfortable with the accent, so that it sits in your mouth with the same familiarity as when you wear a favourite coat. This is one very good reason to see a dialect coach. There are quite a few of us now and it pays to have that hour's worth of confidence building. Also, if you have been briefed to speak in a specific accent, but are unsure what that means, ask a dialect expert, we understand the 'lingo'. If you are asked to read a script in an accent, on the spot – so to speak – ask for five minutes preparation time and go elsewhere to do this, so that you can practice aloud, not in your head.

Don't use a drama school audition as an 'Accent Show'. They want to hear the potential of your own voice and speech, so only choose to use an accent if you're really 'at home' with it. Try to master a few accents for your repertoire, especially a modern Received Pronunciation (RP). It acts as a physical springboard for all the rest.'

Advice from the Actors

I asked two actors, who have both left drama school within the past five years to give some tips on auditioning and tell us a bit about their own experiences:

Samantha Power trained at the Welsh College of Music and Drama and played 'Cecily' in the Number One Tour of *The Importance of Being Earnest*. On television she has appeared in *City Central*, *Cops* and *Peak Practice* and was 'Sonia' in the BBC Television sitcom *A Prince Among Men*. She also plays 'Lisa' in the film *Low Down* directed by Jamie Thraves.

'Auditions can be quite an intimidating experience, especially in the early stages of your career, but I believe they can often be quite exciting and enjoyable.

When you go up for a television audition you will usually meet the director, casting director and sometimes the producer. You are often required to read from the script so if sight-reading isn't your strong point – Practise!

It is important to find as much information about the role as possible – what the character is like, the general synopsis and style of the piece – all of which will create a clear picture in your mind and help prepare you for the audition. If you haven't had the luxury of being sent a script, make sure you arrive early enough to look through it.

I remember auditioning for a new BBC sitcom just six months out of drama school. I was sent the script in advance and I read it over and over again searching for clues as to what this character was like. I worked on it with the same approach I would any other role. I had the audition and was then recalled to meet the writers and the producer, and to read opposite the well-known lead actor. I was successful. Much later, I was told by one of the writers the reason I got the part was because 'You came into the room and made the character your own!' If you are prepared to work hard you will see the rewards.

If you are required to do a dialect, it is imperative you do it correctly. Any one of the people auditioning you could be from that area, so if you haven't prepared it could turn into a very embarrassing situation!

Always remember, if it doesn't work out the first time, don't be disillusioned. Decisions are based upon several factors. It is not necessarily a reflection on your ability to act!

So think positive. Be patient and Good Luck!'

Matt Plant trained at the Academy Drama School. He recently played 'Algernon' in the Number One Tour of *The Importance of Being Earnest* and 'The Tutor' in *Anger* for BBC Television, directed by David Berry:

'Sometimes one is asked to travel long distances to an audition. This should never deter an actor as it could be 'the crock of gold at the end of the rainbow' and if it's not, you can always turn it down. Either way it can only add to your experience. At least that's what I thought as I walked into the Gaiety Theatre, Ayr in Scotland! I had already travelled all the way up from London by bus, thanks to the unfailing dedication of our beloved rail, had endured the dictates of Mrs Mince's 'Oh yes, all the stars stay here' boarding house, and was prepared for anything.

The audition panel, for it was a panel, wore suits and for a moment I thought perhaps I was being interviewed for Microsoft! 'Sing Happy Birthday', they said. 'What for?' I exclaimed, this being an audition for Terence Rattigan's *Murder in Mind*. I should have known when they asked if I could 'act like a mole' and 'talk like a farmer', and at this point produced a horse's head (papier mâché). It was only later I realised they had been considering me for 'future projects', whatever those projects were, and in actual fact the Rattigan play had already been cast!

The experience did not put me off auditions, or travelling long distances to get to them, although it has given me a strange aversion to horses! Funny that . . .'

Auditioning for Films and Television

Even the most experienced actors will often tell you they have no idea why they got a particular film or television part or, why they didn't. What are film and television directors looking for? I was once told at a screen test, as I fumbled with the script I had just been handed by the casting director and tried to read it, at her request, without my glasses, 'Don't worry – it's really a 'look' they're looking for'!

So I passed this problem over to film and television casting director, **Doreen Jones**, who cast the film *Orphans* for Peter Mullins, the television mini-series *Prime Suspect* and is currently working on *The Vice*:

'First thing to remember is that generally speaking (I can only speak for myself) you wouldn't be at the interview unless the casting director thought you were good. Nowadays with a very short run-up to the start of most film and television, there just isn't time to see the world and their mother. Generally I only suggest a few actors for each part but they will have been whittled down from an enormous list. I usually bring in three or four actors who represent different ways of playing the part.

If possible, try and find out a bit about the project. If it's an adaptation of a book, directors are impressed if you've taken the trouble to read the book – it shows commitment. Engage with the people you're meeting – it's no good leaning back in your seat trying to look cool – it looks as if you aren't interested; lean forward and show enthusiasm for the project – but don't go over the top. You may be asked to read – some actors have a facility for this and some don't. In order to give yourself the maximum chance, either arrive earlier so that you can familiarise yourself with the part or call the casting director the day before and ask if you can come in and pick up the lines or have them faxed to you. Only the churlish will refuse. This means that when you do read, you will be able to make eye contact with whoever is reading with you (usually the poor casting director) and again directors will be impressed that you have taken the trouble. Very often the director will say after just reading once, that was just fine. If you're not happy, ask to have one more go and ask if the director would like it a bit differently. Sometimes I would like an actor to have another go, but it's tricky for a casting director to intervene at this point – it could look as if they are undermining the director.

Occasionally you will be sent a script before a meeting. This is because the director finds it helpful to find out what your 'take' is on the script. So read it properly, not just once but several times so that you can talk intelligently and in depth about the character you have come in for. Make a note of not only the writer's notes and what your character says but also what other characters say about you. Do not, on any account arrive saying you didn't have time to read it properly. If that's the case, you might as well leave then because it's unlikely you'll get the part. If something catastrophic has happened in your personal life, and you genuinely have not been able to read the script, get on to your agent and see if you can be seen later. If you have had the script you should definitely learn the lines, not necessarily to the extent that you can put the script away but enough so that you don't have to constantly refer to it.

There are still some directors around who don't read actors. It may be that they prefer to rely on their 'gut' instinct or that they and the casting director have worked together many times and know each other's taste. In these cases it sometimes helps to talk about parts that you have played (subtly of course!) that may bear some resemblance to the character you have come in for. If you have come in for a character with an accent that is not your normal accent it is a good idea to think of a story to tell which involves you using the accent of that character.

There are lots of 'Chiefs' around these days and sometimes it is necessary when we 'Indians' have made a decision about who we would like to play the part, that we have to refer it upwards. This is when you will be asked back to go on video. So please think about the part you are videoing for. Don't have a late night if you're going to look wrecked the next day and that's not what the part calls for. It will be the first time the executives have seen you and no amount of us saying that you really are only twenty-three even if you're looking forty will convince them that we have made the right decision. You will not only have let yourself down, you will have let down those who had confidence in you as well.

When you don't get the part, try not to take it too personally. Remember that you wouldn't have been in for the interview if the casting director didn't think you were a good actor. More than likely, the decision will have been made on physical grounds i.e. family resemblance or a physical variation within a group so that the audience can distinguish one character from another.'

Auditioning for Voiceovers and Radio Drama

Patricia Leventon, Royal Shakespeare Company actress and former member of the BBC Radio Drama Company:

'Your voice can be your fortune. A good flexible voice coupled with the ability to sight-read is one of the greatest assets an actor can have. The world of commercial voiceovers both on radio and TV can be extremely lucrative. You have to be able to go into a studio, pick up a script, read it, time it and give the exact emphasis required by the advertiser. Often there are a great many words needing all your articulatory skills to fit them into the ten, twenty or thirty seconds of the average commercial.

Radio Drama is another great source of work. Most of the drama schools now enter their students for the Carlton Hobbs Award (named after the great radio actor of the 1940s, '50s and '60s). This competition takes place towards the end of the academic year, i.e. June, and six students are awarded a place with the BBC Radio Drama Company. They provide a talent base and are usually given a six-month contract enabling them to gain experience of the medium and supplying them with the opportunity to work alongside very experienced actors in the field. For these auditions it is advisable for students to work on their pieces in detail with their tutor as much in advance as possible. Choose pieces you feel at home with. The usual contrast of comedy and drama is expected. Also classical and modern. Only use native accents if you want to use a dialect. There are a great many actors around from America, Ireland, Scotland, Wales etc. And it is not sensible to put yourself in competition with the real thing.

If you're fortunate enough to work with BBC Radio then again the ability to pick up a script and 'lift' the part off the page is a 'must'. For an afternoon play or a longer work on Radio 3 you will get a script with sufficient time to study your part. Raising your eyes off the script and making contact with the other actors or looking straight into the microphone to express your inner emotions and thoughts are the beauty of radio work and are very satisfying for the actor. Radio is experiencing a renaissance in this new Millennium. Long may it continue.

The spoken word is important and the recording field is vast. There are numerous Talking Books, Shakespearean CDs, language tapes, children's cassettes, all giving opportunities to the vocally well equipped actor.

If you love a particular book and have an ambition to read it and as far as you know it hasn't been recorded recently it is worthwhile doing a bit of research to find out if any of the publishers who have media departments would be interested. They'll probably want a 'star name' but it is worth a go.

Simple voice exercises keep the voice in trim and these should be done gently every day. Don't lose your original accent as it is useful for television drama, soaps etc. but work at Received Pronunciation for the opportunity to work in classical drama. Keep reading and above all enjoy.'

Carol Schroder LLAM is an Examiner for the London Academy of Music and Dramatic Art (LAMDA) and an experienced teacher of drama and performing arts. She is the author of several textbooks.

'This is an imaginative, exciting and well researched collection of scenes. Whilst using some well known sources there is a wealth of material from new writers representing plays that have been performed in a variety of theatres from the fringe to the West End and other countries.

The scenes offer scope to actors of all ages and experience and will equip them with a range of material that will admirably demonstrate their versatility, either for auditions or examinations. Many are taken from plays written since 1985 and this is an essential criteria of the syllabus requirements for the LAMDA medal examinations.

It is always rewarding to discover new material, especially that which will challenge the actor and give pleasure both in the preparation and the performance.'

A Word About the Speeches

Each of the following speeches has its own introduction, giving the date of the original production – information often required for auditions and drama examinations – a few lines about the play itself, and the scene leading up to the actual speech. Even so, it is important to read the whole play. Not only will you most probably be asked questions such as, 'What happened in the previous scene?' but also the other characters in the play can give you vital information about your character.

At the top left hand corner of each introduction I have, where possible, given the age, or approximate age of the character, and their nationality, and/or the region or area they come from. If a region or nationality is not mentioned then standard English, RP (Received Pronunciation), or your own voice should be used. When a play is in translation, or is set in another country, only characters foreign to that particular country need to use an accent or dialect. The characters in Maxim Gorky's *Summerfolk* would not be speaking in Russian voices any more than those in *Oroonoko* need to use African voices. In other words – use your own voice. No funny accents! Here again, reading the whole play should give you a better idea of whether the character is suited to you.

AUDITION SPEECHES
for WOMEN

LINDSAY
mid 30s

THE ABSENCE OF WAR
David Hare

First produced at the Olivier Theatre in 1993 as part of the Royal
National Theatre's David Hare trilogy. This is the third part of the
trilogy about British institutions and it looks at the way politicians
think and act today and the problems that beset them.

After a long period of turmoil, the Leader's office has imposed an
uneasy period of calm on the Labour Party. But the leader, George
Jones, knows he has only one chance of power. LINDSAY FONTAINE
is George's new publicity adviser. She is described as articulate and
quick thinking. George's minder, Andrew Buchan and his political
adviser, Oliver Dix, are both uneasy over the appointment. George
himself is unperturbed.

The election is going badly and LINDSAY wants to hold an
emergency meeting. Andrew says that they've been trying to intro-
duce properly organised meetings and this is not the time to let that
discipline go. George insists that LINDSAY speaks her mind.

Published by Faber & Faber, London

LINDSAY

You see, George, from the beginning, I've had a real problem. The first time I met you, I thought, here's this extraordinary man. In private, articulate, funny, authoritative. Yet who tightens up the minute he goes public, the minute he talks policy.

(Andrew *has sat down on the edge of the table.* Gwenda *is standing over* George.)

So the first thing I did was begin to look around you. It's obvious, really. I began to talk to your team. And it's like . . . I don't know . . . it was like they'd forgotten, it was clear they'd lost sight of who you really are.

(Andrew *looks across to* George.)

. . . No, everything they said, it was as if they were trying to protect you. I found I developed that protective mentality myself. (*She smiles at George.*) I started to see you as a sort of patient in hospital. And like the rest of us I started to behave like I was a nurse. . . . I know it's cowardly to say this when Oliver's not here. But he does create a certain atmosphere. . . . He creates a nervousness, and I have to say that nervousness has taken its toll.

(George *is watching, giving nothing away.*)

That night in the studio, I watched you, I realized . . . way before Linus Frank did his trick . . . I thought, this man is trapped. He can only convey one message to the nation: 'Oh God, I hope I don't drop a bollock tonight . . .'

(Andrew *shakes his head.*)

. . . Oh yes, you explained to me. George once made a blunder, what was it, six years ago . . . ? . . . and for that you still want to punish him. You decided for some reason to smother his wit. All his gaiety. His humour.

(Andrew *turns away, angry now.*)

. . . And that's why he's angry. Underneath George is always bloody furious. He's angry. And who can blame him?

(George *watches, giving nothing away.*)

Everything in him wants to let rip.

(Andrew *looks to* George, *but* LINDSAY *goes straight on.*)

The public aren't stupid. They know he's been programmed. It's not hard to work out why this man's ratings are low. The public see only one thing when they look at him, and that's six rolls of sticky tape wrapped round his mouth . . .

(*She turns, indignant now.*)

What's wrong with us? Are we really so cynical . . . are we so arrogant, that we truly imagine the public can't tell?

ALBERTINE AT 30
30

ALBERTINE IN FIVE TIMES
Michel Tremblay
Translated by John Van Burek and Bill Glassco

First performed in this country at the Donmar Warehouse, London by the Tarragon Theatre, Toronto in 1986.

ALBERTINE is performed by five different actresses at successive ages in the character's life – thirty, forty, fifty, sixty and seventy. All five talk to each other freely and also to ALBERTINE's sister, Madeleine.

ALBERTINE AT 30 is recuperating after viciously beating her eleven year old daughter, Thérèse. In this scene she is trying to explain to Madeleine and the other Albertines the rage she feels inside that led her to attack her own child.

Published by Nick Hern Books, London

ALBERTINE AT 30
I'm young, I'm strong, I could do so much if it weren't for this rage, gnawing at me . . . Sometimes I think it's all that keeps me alive . . . I'll tell you why I'm here this week, Madeleine, you'll understand . . . You'll understand what I mean by this rage.
(*Silence. The other* Albertines *and* Madeleine *listen carefully.*)
My child, my own daughter, my Thérèse, who I fight with all the time because we're so alike . . . though I try to bring her up as best I can . . . It's true, you know, I do the best I can . . . I don't know much, but what I do know I try to pass on to my kids . . . though they never listen. Another thing that enrages me . . . Anyway . . . my Thérèse who I always thought was so innocent, with her dolls and those girlfriends she leads around by the nose . . . Believe it or not, she was seeing a man. A man, Madeleine, not some brat her own age who'd be happy to kiss her with her mouth closed, but a grown man! . . . Eleven years old, Madeleine, and he was chasing her like she was a woman! Following her everywhere. And she let him do what he liked, without

a word. She knew, and she didn't say a word! . . . She liked it, Madeleine, she told me herself. And that's why I beat her. . . . Naturally I found out by accident. I was lying on the sofa the other day, in the middle of the afternoon . . . I could feel a storm brewing . . . Mother'd been in a rotten mood all day, the kids were driving me nuts . . . Thérèse came to sit on the front balcony with her friend Pierrette.

(*Silence.*)

They talked about it like it was an everyday thing . . . Pierrette asked Thérèse if she'd seen her 'gent' lately and she said he disappeared the beginning of June. I assumed it was some neighbourhood kid, and I figured: 'Here we go, boy problems. Already.' Then I realized it wasn't that at all. They were talking about him like he was an actor, for God's sake. Comparing him to those movie stars in the magazines . . . They even said he was better looking! I lay there, horrified . . . They had no idea . . . of the danger . . . the danger of men, Madeleine . . . And when Thérèse started talking about the last time she saw him, how he got down on his knees in front of her right on the street and put his head on . . . her belly, I got up, not knowing what I was doing and went out on the balcony . . . and I started to hit her, Madeleine. . . . I didn't know where I was hitting. I just hit her as hard as I could. Thérèse was screaming, Pierrette was crying, the neighbours coming out of their houses . . . and I didn't stop . . . I couldn't. It wasn't just Thérèse I was hitting, it was . . . my whole life . . . I couldn't find the words to explain the danger, so I just hit! (*She turns toward her sister.*) I never told Thérèse much about men 'cause the words would have been filthy. (*Silence.*) If Gabriel hadn't come out and separated us, I would have killed her.

(Madeleine *puts her hand on her sister's shoulder who throws herself into her arms.*)

I didn't cry, Madeleine. Not once. And I still can't. (*Silence.*) Rage.

An excerpt (abridged) from *Albertine in Five Times*
by Michel Tremblay.
Translated by John Van Burek and Bill Glassco.
Published by Nick Hern Books, The Glasshouse, 49a Goldhawk Road, London W12 8QP.

19

CAROLINE
German
late 20s

BATTLE ROYAL
Nick Stafford

First performed on the Lyttleton stage of the Royal National Theatre in December 1999.

The play follows the events of the tempestuous marriage of George IV and his outspoken wife, CAROLINE of Brunswick – from their first disastrous meeting in 1795 prior to the wedding, through their inevitable separation and his failed attempt to divorce her for adultery, to her death in 1821.

In this opening scene CAROLINE has been summoned to London from Brunswick. The Prince Regent is under pressure to marry and CAROLINE, whose mother is the King's sister, is considered the most suitable candidate. She is standing impatiently in a room in the palace whilst her maid, Mariette, is attempting to prepare her for this first important meeting.

Published by Faber & Faber, London

CAROLINE

I cannot sit still any more, I cannot sit at all – . . . And I must pace and I must fidget. Oh my heartbeat, oh my breath – ow! Yes. Good. Here. I am still. No. Still enough? Good. God, help me through this ordeal. Here I am, then. Here we are. In England. Summoned from an outpost. Me. Here I am. See his picture? (*locket*) . . . 'Here,' said kind Lord Malmesbury, 'this is his portrait.' Isn't Lord Malmesbury a true English gentleman? . . . What a land if they all resemble him – which they don't, of course. . . . Goodbye, mother; goodbye, father. So proud he's chosen me. 'Oh my God!,' my mother said. 'The Prince of Wales seeks your hand? I do not dare to believe.' The line of carriages; goodbye, goodbye Brunswick – goodbye! Head for the sea. This way, that way. A diversion! Napoleon's troops reported over there! Camp here. Wait for escort. Here. Go on. Safe now. To the ship. And Malmesbury, so attentive: 'Perhaps, Ma'am, perhaps I may show you how the Prince conducts himself at the dinner table. Like so. And so. And so.' . . . And ahoy! ahoy! the white cliffs, and first foot in England. Where's this? Who's that? – . . . Be still, be still, both you and Lord Malmesbury tell me be still, and: 'Be dignified, Ma'am, look ahead, be dignified, demure, aloof even.' Aloof? aloof? English words – but they all look at me, they all whisper: where is she? is that her? And I want to shout yes! it is me! here I am! But I am aloof, demure, yes, Lord Malmesbury, I am sorry, Lord Malmesbury – ow!

MARIE
Belfast
30s

BOLD GIRLS
Rona Munro

First performed at the Cumberland Theatre, Strathclyde in 1991.

The play depicts the lives of three women, MARIE, Cassie and Nora in war-torn Belfast. Although their men have been killed or imprisoned for political activities, life still has to go on.

This scene is set in MARIE's kitchen. Here, almost at the beginning of the play, she is preparing bread for the birds as she talks about her brother, Davey and her husband, Michael and his friends.

Published by Hodder & Stoughton, London

MARIE

I like the pigeons. I saw a pigeon fly across the sky and when it crossed the clouds it was black but when it flew past the roofs it was white. It could fly as far as it liked but it never went further than Turf Lodge from what I could see. (*Pause*) I used to watch for that bird, the only white bird that wasn't a seagull. (*Pause*) He wasn't even the man they wanted, but they shot him; that made him the man they wanted. (*Pause*) You have to imagine the four of them. All men you'd look at twice one way or another. Michael, my husband, because he had that strong feel to him. You felt it in the back of your neck when he came in a room. People turned to look without knowing why. Davey, my brother now, you'd look again but you'd say, what's that wee boy doing in his daddy's jacket. Nineteen and he looks more like nine, though they've put age in his eyes for him now. He's got old eyes now. Martin, Cassie's brother, you'd look and you'd cross the street in case he caught your eye and decided he didn't like the look of *you*, he's got the kind of eyebrows that chop short conversations, slamming a glower on his face like two fists hitting a table – and Joe, Cassie's husband. You'd look at him to see what the joke was, Joe's always laughing. Joe's always where the crack is. (*Pause*) Davey's in the Kesh. Martin's in the Kesh. Joe's in the Kesh – and Michael is dead. (*Pause*) They didn't really go round together, the four of them, just every odd Saturday they'd be in here playing cards till they were three of them broke and Joe stuffed with beer and winnings. Singing till they were too drunk to remember the words then waking and eating and drinking some more till they were drunk enough to make up their own. Sure it was a party they had. And Davey felt like a man and Martin smiled and Joe sang almost in tune and Michael would tell me he loved me over and over till he'd made a song out of that. (*Pause*) Sometimes he said he loved me when he'd no drink in him at all. Sometimes he even did that.

An excerpt (abridged) from *Bold Girls* by Rona Munro.
Published by Hodder & Stoughton, London
Reproduced by permission of Nick Hern Books, The Glasshouse,
49a Goldhawk Road, London W12 8QP.

BEATRICE
20s

THE CLINK
Stephen Jeffreys

First produced by Paines Plough at the Theatre Royal, Plymouth in 1990 and set in and around 'The Clink' – a prison in Southwark, London – towards the end of the reign of Elizabeth the First.

BEATRICE is Lady in Waiting to Queen Elizabeth. Her father, a privy councillor to the Queen, has arranged for her to marry Martin Gridling, a man she heartily despises. Her maid, Zanda, devises a plot to get rid of Gridling who is a well known 'roarer'. The girls disguise themselves as 'roaring girls' and invite him to a duel at dawn. BEATRICE easily wins this duel of words, then takes a pistol from her cloak and shoots him dead. The blame is laid on the innocent Lucius Bodkin who had been persuaded to act as Gridling's second.

In this scene BEATRICE, covered in mud, is sitting on the floor of her room while Zanda brushes out her hair. She is in ecstasy over the murder. Zanda says she must conceal her crime for both their sakes, but when her father arrives home she can't wait to tell him how she shot her husband-to-be through the heart with silver bullets.

Published by Nick Hern Books, London

BEATRICE
I see his face. A piece of parchment scratched on by a child and left out in the rain. The mud of London's fields spattering his eyes and nose. Mud on my boots. After killing, every action so loud. I tug at a broken nail, the rip of it deafens me. Again and again I feel the jolt of the pistol in my hand. The ease of it. The ecstasy. . . .
(BEATRICE *stands suddenly. The hairbrush drops to the floor.*)
I have snapped a link in the chain of being, a small snip to a link and now the chain is sundered, and what is outside the chain? They told me hell, and they told me falsely. I killed but I am not in the furnace. I am in the thrilling region, the realm of ice where the air is dizzy. . . . I have their secret! I know the secret the men have, that they carry

24

with them, which gives them power! The swords on their hips, their furtive pistols. Killing is exciting, it is power. You knew that from your slave days and yet you kept it from me. . . . Now I am delivered. I am no longer one who waits, looks on and nods agreement. I change the face of the earth. I squeeze a trigger and the world is changed. There is nothing I cannot do! . . . I am a killer. I am one of them. . . . They put a prayer book in my hand and told me God would see my every sin. But I have done the worst, the final sin and am not seen. I have not put myself in prison, I have burst out. You talk of freedom here on earth, freedom of the body, when I speak of my eternal soul. . . .

(Warburton, *her father, comes in. He wears the chain of office.*)

Shot. Through the heart. Silver bullets. In the mud beyond Edgware. . . . I have the pistol here. And here the murderer's hand. . . . Father, I have not thanked you for my education. . . . Not for the Latin and Greek whipped into me, but for your education in the art of politic murder. For did you not show me the way with friend Frobisher, did you not send the Bishop and Lord Davenport to the axe. But there is a fault I find in my killing education, that I must go to finishing school at the feet of our slave. You taught me only the grammar and syntax of murder, but Zanda rendered me the gift of tongues – . . . she put the pistol in my hand and gave me the trigger lesson. I shot the man you wanted for my husband and now I stand forever free. . . . I am let loose for ever. . . .

(*She threatens them with the pistol.*)

I cannot be confined within my prayer book room. I am now out among the world. There is no chain you can devise that will ever drag me back. I was never innocent. I watched the worms eating at the stair and, in my secret thoughts, considered them good. But now I take a hatchet to the banisters and smile.

(BEATRICE *goes.*)

An excerpt (abridged) from *The Clink* by Stephen Jeffreys.
Published by Nick Hern Books, The Glasshouse, 49a Goldhawk Road, London W12 8QP.

ZANDA
Originally from Morocco
20s

THE CLINK
Stephen Jeffreys

First produced by Paines Plough at the Theatre Royal, Plymouth in 1990 and set in and around 'The Clink' – a prison in Southwark, London – towards the end of the reign of Elizabeth the First.

ZANDA is a slave shipped over from Morocco and bought by privy councillor Warburton to look after his daughter, Beatrice, who is Lady in Waiting to the Queen. Warburton has arranged for his daughter to marry Martin Gridling, a man she heartily despises. ZANDA devises a plot to get rid of him. Gridling is a well known 'roarer' and the girls disguise themselves as 'roaring girls' and invite him to a duel. Beatrice easily wins this duel of words, then takes a pistol from her cloak and shoots Gridling dead. The blame is laid on the innocent Lucius Bodkin who had been persuaded to act as Gridling's second.

In this scene Beatrice, covered in mud, is musing happily over the murder she has just committed. ZANDA tries to persuade her to come to bed. They need sleep. The murder must be concealed from her father at all costs and tomorrow they must act their innocence.

Published by Nick Hern Books, London

ZANDA

My lady. Will you come to bed? It is time. . . . We will act the perfect maid and lady and follow daily customs. Your father must harbour no suspicion against us. I will brush your hair and soothe you, then you'll sleep. . . . Tomorrow we will fetch water to wash it. Now sit. . . . You are the mistress in the house, but I am Queen in the streets and we have brought the street stink here into your chambers. You do not know what musks and mists can cover murder but I do and you will swallow my prescription. Now sit.

(Beatrice *sits on the floor, but not where* ZANDA *has indicated.*

ZANDA *goes to her and brushes.*)

When I was a slave to the Spaniards, I was their thing to use as they wished. I fetched for them, skivvied. They took me, sleeping, in sickness, they didn't care. One was the ship's doctor. He grabbed me, sudden while I slept upon the deck. I turned and fisted him, he fell, heavy, his head striking a cannon. Dead. I held his body up and nailed it to the mast. The crew looked on. They never troubled me again. I said: 'Now I am your doctor.' I had broken the chain. . . . As you have broken yours. . . . You have freed yourself. . . . You wait. You live from day to day. You relish the snapping of your chain. . . . I meant the chain that bound you to your father. . . . You must not trumpet out this murder. Your father will be high in anger at this death and you must play bereavement to the hilt. . . . The Queen grows sicker. This is the report from every stair and corridor. When she is dead, your power in the court is gone. All you can ever be is a drain on your father's exchequer or a quim for trading on the market. You have 'scaped one husband, you cannot 'scape them all. . . .

(ZANDA *seizes* Beatrice.)

You and I have been as sisters! We have brought the two halves of the globe together and made a safe cocoon to live in, an egg where we have dwelt in safety from the world of men. The shell is shattered now. We must stand together. Without me you will have no access to the world of pleasure and die a country death with a fat husband. Without you I have no privilege and cannot be protected from the curs who call me blackamoor and spit upon my skin. . . . You must conceal this murder. If you broadcast it abroad, my complicity will be much blamed. . . . Your guilt, once known will be laden at my door.

An excerpt (abridged) from *The Clink* by Stephen Jeffreys.
Published by Nick Hern Books, The Glasshouse,
49a Goldhawk Road, London W12 8QP.

MARGO BOYE-ANAWOMA
(A Lawyer)
DOREEN LAWRENCE
Black
early middle-age

THE COLOUR OF JUSTICE
Based on the Transcripts of the Stephen Lawrence Inquiry
Edited by Richard Norton-Taylor

First performed at the Tricycle Theatre in January, 1999 and later transferred to the Victoria Palace, London.

This is a dramatic reconstruction of the hearings which erupted into national outrage when black teenager, Stephen Lawrence was stabbed to death by a gang of white youths, and the police investigation failed to provide sufficient evidence to convict.

In this extract lawyer MARGO BOYE-ANAWOMA continues to read DOREEN LAWRENCE's statement at the Inquiry. DOREEN, Stephen's mother, is sitting next to her throughout the hearing. The statement describes her frustrated attempts to obtain justice for her son leading up to the Lawrences' decision to begin a private prosecution. This extract could also be played as DOREEN LAWRENCE herself making her statement.

Published by Oberon Books, London

BOYE-ANAWOMA
I am going to carry on reading MRS LAWRENCE's statement.
  (*Reads statement.*)
'The police were not interested in keeping us informed about the investigation. We were simply regarded as irritants.

'It was also claimed that the police found dealing with our solicitor a hindrance. Basically, we were seen as gullible simpletons. This is best shown by Ilsley's comment that I had obviously been primed to ask questions. Presumably, there is no possibility of me being an intelligent, black woman with thoughts of her own who is able to ask questions for herself. We were patronised and we were fobbed off. As the meetings went on, I got more and more angry. I thought that the purpose of the meetings was to give us progress reports, but what actually happened was that they would effectively say: stop questioning us. We are doing everything. That simply was not true, and it led me to believe then and now that they were protecting the suspects.

'The second investigation started with meeting Commissioner Condon in April 1994. We discussed the Barker review, and that was the first time we met Ian Johnston. We were still kept in the dark about some things in the second investigation. We weren't told exactly what was happening, but we heard rumours that things had gone wrong with the first investigation, and I think there was some cover-up about what was going on. It was then decided that the Crown Prosecution Service wouldn't take matters further. I felt we had no choice but to take a private prosecution, and I don't believe they would have been acquitted if we could have presented everything to the jury. On the first day at the Old Bailey I was extremely optimistic, but from the minute the judge opened his mouth, my hopes were dashed. It was clear from the outset he had come with the intention of not letting the matter proceed further. The judge instructed them to return a verdict of not guilty. When he told them that there was no alternative they actually went outside to consider it and then came back in. They didn't want to do it.

' . . . At the beginning the Kent Police Complaints Authority Report was saying that the police officers were not racist in their attitude. If it wasn't racism what was it? Incompetence? Corruption? . . .

'I would like Stephen to be remembered as a young man who had a future. He was well loved and had he been given the chance to survive maybe he would have been the one to bridge the gap between black and white; he just saw people as people.' (*Statement ends.*)

CARLA
age unknown – possibly 30s/40s

COMIC POTENTIAL
Alan Ayckbourn

First performed at the Stephen Joseph Theatre, Scarborough in 1998 and at the Lyric Theatre, London in 1999, it is set in the foreseeable future when everything has changed except human nature.

CARLA PEPPERBLOOM is the Regional Director of a commercial television company producing TV soaps using android actors. A woman of uncertain age, she is used to having her own way and has a reputation for taking up with young men, known in the company as the 'Pepperbloom Babes'. She arrives at the studios with Adam Trainsmith, a young writer and nephew of the Chairman, who is anxious to study television technique with Chance Chandler, a director he has long admired. Adam is fascinated by the 'actoids' and persuades Chance to let him try out an idea of his own.

In this scene CARLA announces that she has made arrangements for them to fly over to Paris together. Adam tells her this is impossible. Chance has promised him the use of the studio and he needs to take advantage of his offer. CARLA is furious and proceeds to teach Adam the 'facts of television life'.

Published by Faber & Faber, London

CARLA

Adam, dear, you badly need to learn the facts of television life. This is not how you go about things. If you want to make a programme, the first thing you do is submit the idea in writing to our storyline department. If they approve it, then they will pass it on to our script department. Storyline have a big backlog at present so this can take up to six months. In turn, the script department will then consider it and if they're enthusiastic – and they also have a huge backlog, so add another six months at least – they will contact you and suggest you develop your idea to what we call PFS, the Primary Full Synopsis. This is unpaid and there is no guarantee at the end of it that the idea will go forward from there. But assuming it's approved, and that's a very big if, because the competition is frightening, you will be asked to meet an editor who will talk it through with you and all being well and if they're happy, you will receive a down payment commissioning a first draft. Scripts can go to four or five drafts, generally more. This process can take anything up to two years. At the end of this time, if we can find an interested director, the piece might actually be made. Though I should warn you that for every hundred scripts that reach their final draft stage, only fifteen are made and of those usually five are shelved before transmission. And unless it's transmitted, under the new agreements, you will not, of course, receive your full and final fee. Welcome to modern television, Adam.
. . . You stand no chance at all because I won't allow it to happen.
. . . Because I am the overall Regional Director here, Adam, and things are done my way. And I don't care if you're the chairman's mistress, you can bloody well toe the line like everybody else, now are you coming?

JACIE
seemingly 19

COMIC POTENTIAL
Alan Ayckbourn

First performed at the Stephen Joseph Theatre, Scarborough in 1998 and at the Lyric Theatre, London, in 1999, it is set in the foreseeable future when everything has changed except human nature.

JACIE is an 'actoid' – one of the androids manufactured to replace human actors and programmed to perform in TV soaps. A young writer, Adam Trainsmith, despite warnings from the studio technicians, has befriended JACIE and persuades the series director to let him write and produce a soap with JACIE in the leading role. His project is going well until Carla Pepperbloom, the Regional Director of the TV Company, turns down the idea and the Chairman condemns JACIE to be taken back to the factory and melted down. Determined to save JACIE, Adam runs away with her.

In this scene set in a sleazy hotel room, Adam tells JACIE he loves her. She is confused and upset and reminds him that she is, after all, only a machine.

Published by Faber & Faber, London

JACIE

I am not Jacie, Adam. I am JCF 31 triple 3. There is no Jacie. There's no real me. I'm a machine, Adam. I wasn't taught to think of myself as that, but I acknowledge now that I am. On the one hand, it's a fact that every day we stay together, you'll change and I'll stay the same. I'm nineteen years old and I have been like this since the day I was made. . . . Adam, you must listen. Don't laugh at me. I'm trying to say something and it's difficult for me. . . . But on the other hand, despite that, I will only ever be what people want me to be. I'll be a nurse or a soldier or a runaway bride or grumpy woman in tea shop. But I can never be me. So I can't do what you want me to. You're asking too much of me, Adam. Yes, I can *play* your Jacie. I can play her just as you want her to be. I'm good at that. That's what I was made for. But I can never *be* your Jacie. Do you see the difference? I've been mis-cast, you see. Please. Take me back. Audition failed. Leave your name at the door. We'll keep in touch. . . . (*increasingly agitated*) I want to go back, I want to melt down. I don't want to be like this any more. It's too painful. Nothing's working. I can't control me. Look at me, I'm crying and I have no stimulus to cry. I'm so unhappy, Adam. You don't know how I feel . . . You can't know! If you knew and if you loved me, you wouldn't let this happen to me. . . . (*in a quite uncontrolled fury*) This is not a programme. This is me talking, Adam. And I'm lost and I don't know what I'm doing and nobody's telling me and the only person in the world that I trust is standing there talking to me like a child. And I refuse to be treated like that, do you hear me? You make plans for our future without consulting me, you dress me up like some mindless puppet, you humiliate me in shops and restaurants, move me in and out of hotel rooms and make me feel like a second-hand trollop and then you won't even make an effort to understand what I'm trying to tell you – well, you can just go to hell and screw yourself and see if I care, you – stupid fuck dyke!

(*Silence.* JACIE *stands breathless from her outburst.*)
Was that me? . . . Oh God.

ELEONORA
young

EASTER
August Strindberg
Translated by Peter Watts

First performed at the Intima Teatern, Stockholm in 1901 and in Katie Mitchell's production for the Royal Shakespeare Company in The Pit at the Barbican in 1995, it is set in the small provincial town of Lund over Easter.

ELEONORA is a young sensitive girl who has just returned from the Asylum, where she was being treated for a mental breakdown. Her father is serving a prison sentence for embezzlement and the family are haunted by creditors.

In this scene she is talking to Benjamin - a young schoolboy who is staying with them and taking private tuition with her brother. She describes how on her way back from the Asylum she broke into a flower shop that was closed for Confirmation Day and took a daffodil in a pot as a present for her brother, leaving a krona and her card on the counter.

Published by Penguin Classics, London

ELEONORA

Shall I tell you about the flowers? Do you know that when I was ill, they made me take a drug made out of henbane which has the power of turning your eyes into magnifying-glasses - Now, belladonna makes you see everything smaller. Anyhow, now I can see much farther than anyone else - I can even see the stars in broad daylight. . . . The stars are always there. I'm facing north now, and I can see Cassiopeia like a great 'W' in the Milky Way. Can you see it? . . . Make a note of that, then: some people can see things that others can't - so don't be too sure of your own eyes. Now I'll tell you about this flower on the table; it's a daffodil, and they come from Switzerland. It has sucked the sunlight into its cup - that's what makes it so yellow, and that's how it can soothe pain. I saw it as I passed a flower-shop just now, and I wanted it for a present for my brother Elis, but when I tried to get in, I found the door was locked, because it's Confirmation Day. I simply had to have the flower, though, so I took out my keys and tried them, and - would you believe it? - my latch-key fitted, so I went in. Now, you know about the silent language of flowers? Well, every scent expresses a whole multitude of thoughts, and all those thoughts came flooding in on me; so with my magnifying eye, I looked into their laboratories where no one has ever seen before, and they told me about the pain that the clumsy gardener had caused them - I won't call him cruel, because he was only thoughtless. And then I left a krona on the counter, with my card, and I took the flower and went.

TAMARA
29

THE EDITING PROCESS
Meredith Oakes

First performed at the Royal Court Theatre, London in 1994 and set in a London publishing company in the 1990's.

In publicity beware of everyone, especially your friends. Swept by the cold winds of change toward a risky corporate future, the editorial staff of *Footnotes in History* engage in a desperate battle for survival. TAMARA DEL FUEGO has been brought in by Lionel, the General Manager of the parent publishing company, to transform the company's fortunes with a new corporate image. She has already vastly overspent her budget and has become involved with Ted, the assistant editor. Together they were responsible for a tin of oysters being spilt over the computer while they were having sex in the photocopying room.

In this scene she meets Eleanor walking along the corridor towards her. Eleanor has only just joined the company as a trainee, but TAMARA knows it is important to keep in with her as her uncle is on the Board.

Published by Oberon Books, London

TAMARA

My computer's down, Eleanor.... Do you want to see your new letter-head? It's gorg. *(Eleanor looks)* Go on, tell me you love it, it's a mock-up obviously, the editor's name goes there, we can put that in later in order to avoid any uncertainty.... Isn't it beautiful.... That's exactly what I was aiming for, timeless is the next big thing. What's your game plan, Eleanor? When I was your age I had the next ten years mapped out. Well I still am your age.... Sometimes I think what I do is actually therapy, you know? Helping companies through a crisis of identity? Because there's no such thing as a bad company. We're talking a confused company, with myself as the medium through which this company can be released. The company talks to me and I listen. I help the company to express what was previously perhaps too obvious for anyone to mention. When I encourage a company to create its new corporate image, that's like a rite of passage for that company, it achieves a deeper awareness of what it wants to project, and I give it the tools it needs to define itself. So it becomes a sort of celebration, a coming of age or a wedding feast, where money should be no object. Should it.... Anyway Lionel told this company I'd be mega. They're not expecting the Seven Wise Virgins. Hostess to a concept is what I am. Well of course the company's given me a budget and I've totally overspent it, and I think everyone should feel they've had a wonderful blow-out and that it's a really special time. I mean I hope your uncle will understand. Perhaps you could have a talk with him. If you're interested, the girl that does my office is having a baby and I'm going to have to replace her, I didn't realize I was harbouring a breeder, I don't pay much but it isn't about pay, ultimately, is it.... Don't think your uncle's going to do anything for you, the owner only uses him for getting into clubs.... Don't stay too long, this company's dodgier than eggs.

DES-NEIGES
Glaswegian
middle-aged

THE GUID SISTERS

Michel Tremblay

A translation of *Les Belles-Soeurs*

by Bill Findlay and Martin Bowman

Les Belles-Soeurs was first performed in Montreal in 1968 and it's Scots version, *The Guid Sisters* was seen in Glasgow in 1989.

The play is set in the kitchen of a tenement flat where Germaine has won a million premium stamps. These have to be pasted into book before they can be exchanged for goods, and so she has invited her friends and female relatives to a stamp-sticking party. They are jealous of her good fortune and moan about their less fortunate lives. One by one, as they are chatting away they steal the books of stamps, until Germaine notices they are missing and makes them all turn out their bags.

Throughout the action the women are singled out by a spotlight as they reveal their innermost thoughts. DES-NEIGES has been telling the others a dirty joke. Gabrielle remarks that she gets all her jokes from a travelling salesman with whom she is more than 'friendly'. DES-NEIGES protests that there is nothing in their relationship and that she is 'a respectable woman an a good Catholic'. The spotlight is now turned on DES-NEIGES.

Published by Nick Hern Books, London

(*Spotlight on* DES-NEIGES.)

DES-NEIGES

The first time I seen him I thought he was ugly. At least, I didnae think he was guid-looking tae start wi. When I opened the door he took off his hat an said tae me, 'Would the lady of the house be interested in buying some brushes?' I shut the door in his face. I never allows a man intae ma hoose. Ye never know what might happen . . . The only one 'at gets in is the paper boy. He's still owre young tae get any funny ideas. Anyhows, a month later back he came wi his brushes.

It was bucketin ootside so I let him stand in the lobby. Once he was in the hoose, I started tae get jittery, but I tellt masel he didnae look the dangerous type, even if he wasnae very bonny tae look at . . . But he ayeways looks that smart. No a hair oot ae place. Like a real gentleman. And he's ayeways that polite. Well, he selled me a couple ae brushes an then he showed me his catalogue. There was somethin 'at I wanted but he didnae have it wi him so he said I could order it. Ever since then, he's come back once a month. Sometimes I dinnae buy anythin. But he jist comes in an we blether for a wee while. He's an awful nice man . . . I think . . . I really think I'm in love wi him . . . I know it's daft . . . I only see him once a month . . . But it's that nice when we're thegither. I'm that happy when he comes. I've never felt like this afore. It's the first time it's happened tae me. For usual men've never paid me any notice. I've aye been . . . on the shelf, so tae speak. He tells me all aboot his trips, an all kinna stories an jokes. Sometimes his jokes are a wee bit near the bone, but they're that funny! I don't know why, but I've always liked jokes that are a wee bit dirty. It's good for ye, tae, for tae tell dirty jokes noo an again. Mind you, no all his jokes are dirty. Lots ae them are clean. An it's only jist recent he's started tellin me the dirty ones. Sometimes they're that dirty I blush red as a beetroot. The last time he tellt me one he took ma hand cause I blushed. Well, I vernear died. Ma insides went all funny when he put his big hand on mines. I need him sae much! I don't want him tae go away! Sometimes, jist noo an again, I dream aboot him. I dream . . . that we're married. I need him tae come back an see me. He's the first man 'at's ever paid me any notice. I don't want tae lose him! I dinnae want tae lose him! If he goes away, I'll be left on ma own again, and I need . . . somedy tae love . . . *(She lowers her eyes and murmurs)* I need a man.

(The lights come back on)

An excerpt (abridged) from *The Guid Sisters* by Michel Tremblay.
Translated by Bill Findlay and Martin Bowman.
Published by Nick Hern Books, The Glasshouse, 49a Goldhawk Road, London W12 8QP.

LISE
Glaswegian
young

THE GUID SISTERS
Michel Tremblay
A translation of *Les Belles-Soeurs*
by Bill Findlay and Martin Bowman

Les Belles-Soeurs was first performed in Montreal in 1968 and it's Scots version, *The Guid Sisters* was seen in Glasgow in 1989.

The play is set in the kitchen of a tenement flat where Germaine has won a million premium stamps. These have to be pasted into books before they can be exchanged for goods, and so she has invited her friends and female relatives to a stamp-sticking party. They are jealous of her good fortune and moan to each other about their less fortunate lives. One by one they steal the books of stamps until Germaine notices that they are missing and insists that they all turn out their bags. Throughout the action the women are singled out by a spotlight as they reveal their innermost thoughts.

LISE has been brought along to the party by Germaine's daughter, Linda. They are both standing in the spotlight, isolated from the older women, as LISE announces that she is pregnant. They are joined by Pierrette who has overhead the conversation and suggests an abortion. Linda strongly disapproves – 'It's criminal!'

Published by Nick Hern Books, London

LISE

What else would ye have me dae? What choice have I got? It's the
only way oot. I don't want the wean. Look what happened tae Manon
Belair. She was in the same position an noo her life's wasted cause
she's lumbered wi that kid. . . . [The father?] Ye know fine he dropped
us. He beat it soon's he found oot. Naebody seems tae know where
he's went. When I think ae the promises he made us. How happy we
were gaunnae be thegither, an how he was makin money hand-owre-
fist. Eejit that I am. I taen it all in. It was presents here, presents there
. . . there was nae end tae them. Aw, it was nice enough at the time
. . . in fact, it was really nice . . . But bugger it, then this had tae
happen. I jist knew it would. I've never been gien a break. Never.
Why is it me ayeways lands heidfirst in the shite when all I want tae
dae is climb oot ae it? I'm bloody well sick ae workin behind the
counter in that shop. I want tae dae somethin wi ma life. D'ye understand? I want tae get somewhere. I want a car, a nice flat, some nice
claes. Christ knows, aboot all I've got tae put on ma back are shop
overalls. I've aye been hard up . . . aye had tae scrimp'n scrape . . .
But I'm damn sure I'm no gaunnae go on like this. I don't want tae
be a naebody any more. I've had enough ae bein poor. I'm gaunnae
make sure things gets better. I was mebbe born at the bottom ae the
pile but I'm gaunnae climb tae the top. I came intae this world bi
the back door but by Christ I'm gaunnae go oot bi the front. An ye
can take it fae me that nothin's gaunnae get in ma way. Nothin. You
wait, Linda. Jist you wait. You'll see I'm no kiddin. In two three
years you'll see that Lise Paquette's become a somebody. Jist you
watch, she'll be rollin in it then. . . . That's what I'm tryin tae tell
ye. I've made a mistake an I want tae put it right. After that I'm
gaunnae make a new start. You understand what I'm saying, Pierrette,
don't ye?

Excerpt (abridged) from *The Guid Sisters* by Michel Tremblay.
Translated by Bill Findlay and Martin Bowman.
Published by Nick Hern Books, The Glasshouse,
49a Goldhawk Road, London W12 8QP.

CHRISTINE
Midlands
late 30s

HARVEST
Ellen Dryden

First performed at the Birmingham Repertory Studio Theatre in October 1980 and subsequently at the Ambassador's Theatre, London in 1981. It was published in 1996.

The play is set in a small, working-class Midlands village, in a family living within the Methodist church. This is emphasised by the set, which is quickly transformed from chapel into family sitting room. It tells the story of Ted's decision to give up his attempt to get an English degree as a mature student and his sister Marian's efforts to claim her brother for the intellectually liberated world she has moved into.

The opening scene is the funeral service for Marian's granddad, Harry Fenton and changes into the living room where Marian and her sister-in-law, CHRISTINE, are preparing sandwiches for Harry's friends and relations. CHRISTINE is a generous hard-working woman with a deep vein of pessimism which makes her suspicious of everything. She communicates almost the whole time by grumbling and attacking. She has a 'posh' Midlands accent.

Published by First Writes Publications, London

CHRISTINE *(Inspecting a sandwich)*

This ham's all fat! *(She pulls a disgusted face)* Oh, that's nice, isn't it. I told Mom to leave it to me but she wouldn't be said. I expect it's come from the Shop. I think it's disgusting. That great big ham stands there on that cracked plate week in, week out, on the counter – flies buzzing all over it. And Mrs Hollins picks up any old knife to cut it. She can't see beyond her nose-end now, you know. She's always cutting herself. She's never got less than two dirty old plasters on her fingers. Handling food! Then she'll go and serve somebody paraffin and go back to cutting cheese without so much as wiping her fingers. She boils those hams in that old copper, you know, and I wouldn't like to swear that *his* overalls don't go in of a Monday! I told Mom if she wanted ham I could get her some nice wrapped from Marks and Spencers. . . . It would have been the proper shape for sandwiches as well. Look at this!

(She holds out a sandwich with misshapen bits of ham in it)

I mean, when you go to a funeral you don't want to pick up a ham sandwich with bumps in it! I shan't know where to put myself handing these round. . . . *(Tartly)* Well, I'm not proposing to do it on my own. *(Inspecting the rest of the sandwiches)* At least the cheese are a decent shape! But that's only because it's cheese slices – I told her not to get cheese slices. People don't like them. They're all right for convenience, but I don't think they're right for this sort of occasion. I mean it's just not funny, is it? I don't care for Mr Halpern personally but he did go to Cambridge University and I'm sure he'll expect something a bit better than this. . . . I didn't think much of the service anyway. Sitting there like idiots in complete silence. I think he could have thought up *something* a bit nice to say about Granddad. . . . It's his job. Oh my goodness! Don't have a jam tart, Marian. There aren't enough to go round. There's six of this and six of that. Oh, if I'd known what she was up to! . . . *(Vehemently)* You can't get her to do anything properly. You'd think it was still wartime. . . .

Oh! I don't know where Ted's got to. They should be here by now. It's Mrs Ransome keeping them talking, I bet. Getting her pound of flesh – I knew it was a mistake not to invite her to the funeral. She always turns nasty if she doesn't get asked to things.

SUSANNA
Warwickshire
late 20s

THE HERBAL BED
Peter Whelan

First performed by the Royal Shakespeare Company at The Other
Place, Stratford-upon-Avon in 1996 and later at the Barbican Theatre,
London. It transferred to the Duchess Theatre, London in 1997.

The play is based on events that took place in the summer of 1613,
when William Shakespeare's daughter, SUSANNA, married to John
Hall, a respected physician of Stratford, was publicly accused by her
husband's young apprentice of having a sexual liasion with Ralph, a
family friend.

In this scene, SUSANNA tells Ralph that John has guessed at their
relationship, but does not want the truth acknowledged, even to
himself, as this could damage his practice.

Published by Josef Weinberger Plays, London

SUSANNA

He knows already. . . . He's guessed. . . . It's in his look . . . his tone. It's in everything he doesn't say. . . . He knows and mustn't know. He wants our silence. . . . Honesty is not one thing! Love is not one thing . . . nor loyalty . . . he is loyal to his practice and his patients. He's honest in that. And that is his love. And I come second . . . which I accept . . . oh yes! I've seen the terror in the faces of the sick . . . how they reach out to him, their only hope. I can't put myself before that and don't expect him to. So . . . he wants our silence because, if we speak, all that would be shattered like glass . . . Lady Haines would shun him, Lady Rainsford and Underhill . . . the Earl of Northampton . . . and the rest . . . . . . We need the fees of the better off so he can treat the poor. . . . You can't believe that, even in the case of his practice, he would put anything before God himself! That depends what you mean by God himself. If God himself wants the sick to die in pain. If God himself wants plagues and pestilence. If God himself tears children from their parents with their lives unlived . . . as yours were . . . was that God himself? . . . You honour him! . . . How can you honour him by destroying his work? It's only a matter of what you leave out. You came back to tell me that supper was cancelled. I was working in the dispensary. It took a few minutes to tell me. Hester arrived as you were going. . . . If it were left to me I'd leave it. Let it drop. Soon forgotten. Women are slandered every day . . . they're slandered by the hour! Not so much spoken . . . I could walk through Stratford market and be called a whore fifty times over . . . not in words . . . in looks . . . in sneers and nudges. You put on armour against it as a girl and try to wear it lightly. I'm sure worse things have been said. But we must fight it . . . not for ourselves . . . not even for him . . . but for those he might save.

(*As she looks across the garden she sees* Elizabeth *at the cottage.*)

There's Bess . . . playing in the grass. (*She waves to her.*) What a long road we travel . . .

PEARL
Local country accent
20s

HOUSE AND GARDEN
Alan Ayckbourn

First presented at the Stephen Joseph Theatre, Scarborough in 1999 and at the Royal National Theatre on the Olivier and Lyttleton stages in August 2000. *House and Garden* are two plays intended to be performed simultaneously with the same cast appearing in two adjacent auditoria. They can be seen singly and in no particular order. They are about love and marriage and are at the same time funny and sad. This scene is from *Garden*.

Businessman, Teddy Platt and his wife, Trish live in a large country house. Teddy has been having an affair with Joanna, the wife of his friend, Giles, who is also their doctor. Trish has discovered the affair and refuses to speak to or acknowledge her husband. Teddy breaks off the affair with Joanna, who is distraught and having a breakdown. Giles is unaware of the situation. PEARL is a member of the domestic staff and described as a casual cleaner. She is the daughter of their housekeeper, Izzy. Both mother and daughter live with Warn, the gardener and PEARL spends most of her working hours bringing him his lunchbox, or fighting over him with her mother. Warn takes all this for granted.

In this scene PEARL has been comforting Joanna who she found crying in the garden as she brought Warn out his ''levenses'. Giles comes out into the garden and explains that his wife has 'terrible hayfever'. Warn and PEARL stare at him impassively. As he leaves, Warn belches.

Published by Faber & Faber, London

PEARL

He's alright. Poor bloke. She don't know when she's well off. I'd have him. She don't want him, I'd take him off her hands. Bit borin' but not a bad looker. Being a doctor, could be useful, too. Like being married to a plumber. If you spring a leak, he'll fix it for you.

(*Warn is feeling the grass and looking at the sky again.*)

Here. Brought you your 'levenses. Busy today. Got all them people coming to lunch. Doing me silver service. I nearly got it off. 'Less we have sprouts. I'm all over the place with bloody sprouts. I can do carrots. If they're cut long, you know. And beans. I'm alright with beans now. I've mastered beans. Runner beans. Not them broad buggers, they're right bastards. I had 'em everywhere last time. We were pickin' them up for months. I don't know why they don't bung it all on the plate and have done with it. Like normal people.

(*Warn is studying the fountain now.*)

Mum's on the warpath. Been on at me all day. We better not do nothing this year, Warn. She'll be watching us. She can get right barmy, you know that. Like when she went at us with that hot iron, you remember. Bloody lucky it were still plugged in, it could have killed us. Remember? First time she caught us in bed together. Remember? (*She laughs.*) That was a laugh. Still, that were before. It's different now. Circumstances have changed. That's all I'm saying. Know what I mean?

(*Warn appears not to know nor care.*)

I mean, I don't care. Don't matter to me. I never ask anything of anyone. Liberty Hall, I am. But my mum, she . . . Well, anyway. You suit yourself. Be nice to get it settled though, wouldn't it? Get a bit of peace then. You suit yourself, though. It's between you and Mum. Nothing to do with me. I'm easy. I don't care. (*A silence. She reckons she's pursued this tricky topic as much as she can.*) . . .

(*Warn sniffs noisily.*)

Got a film star today. French one. She were in a film. *The Unex* . . . *Unin* . . . *Uninspiring* . . . I don't know. I never seen it. She gets blown up early on. Deirdre told me. But she's good while she lasts. You ought to clean this pond out. It's disgustin'. Breeding ground for things is this. You want to get a stick and clean it out.

NAZREEN
South Asian
young

IN THE SWEAT
Naomi Wallace and Bruce McLeod

This is one of the plays for young people commissioned for New Connections and performed on the Cottesloe and Olivier stages of the Royal National Theatre in 1997.

The action takes place in a disused Synagogue in Spitalfields, London – an area noted for its nonconformity. Four young people, Fitch, an Afro-Caribbean boy, Scudder, a homeless white boy, Duncan, a twenty-one-year-old security guard and NAZREEN, a South Asian girl, are thrown together. The play deals with extreme situations. Their violent confrontation begins to reveal their ties to one another.

Towards the end of the play an elderly Sephardic Jew, Antonio, appears, dragging a stone. NAZREEN recounts the horrific story of her elder sister, traumatised when racists petrol-bombed the phone booth she was in.

From *New Connections – New Plays for Young People*
Published by Faber & Faber, London

NAZREEN

Seven years ago. Yes. Like. Seven hundred. My sister, Mahfuza, and I, we went out to use the phone. To call for flowers. It was my mother's birthday and her favourites were - they were - yes. Mimosa. Small yellow flowers, thin stalks. Mimosa. They smell like dust. Almost sweet. I waited on the corner to make sure my mother did not see us making the call as she walked home from work. Mahfuza was older than me but smaller and had to stand on her toes to put the coins in and dial the number. And then suddenly they were there, three of them, tall, fast boys, who moved quick, quick. Like white flames they sprung up from the stone of the payment. *(Nazreen steps on to the old stone. While she relates the rest of her story, Antonio quietly recites phrases in Portuguese.)* One of them had a can and he circled the phone booth, wetting it like a dog. Another wedged something against the door so my sister could not get out. The third boy, I remember he was laughing but his laugh was strange, almost like crying. He lay broken pieces of wood against the door of the booth and lit the match. And suddenly it seemed the glass of the phone booth started to burn. My sister still had the receiver to her ear, but she was no longer speaking. Her mouth was open. So open. But no sound. And I had started to run towards her. But by then the flames were high and someone grabbed me and held me back. And Mahfuza's mouth was still open behind the flames, as though she were going to eat them. As though she could swallow them whole. And there was smoke, lots of it, and after some moments I could only see the top of Mahfuza's head in the booth, her black hair blacker than the smoke.

The neighbours got her out. In time. What does that mean? In time for what? For months and months after I came home from school I sat with Mahfuza by the window. I wondered if she was looking out for the three young men. Afraid they might come back. But the expression on her face was not one of fear. It was not one of anything. And no matter how many times we bathed her, for years afterwards, her hair still smelled of smoke. It wouldn't wash out. There's nothing wrong with her body but she doesn't walk. There's nothing wrong with her mouth but she doesn't speak. I look at her and I think: 'She is my England.' No, I say. But the hands in her lap, they are cold. 'She is my England.' I say no. Not for me. *(Antonio finishes his recitation.)* For Mahfuza. Perhaps. Yes, for Mahfuza, that silence. Sometimes that's how it happens. But not for me. *(Nazreen takes Antonio's hand in her hand.)* No, not that for me. *(Silence some moments.)* This is it. Here. Right here, isn't it? Under our feet?

STEPH
Northern
20s

INDIAN SUMMER
Lucy Maurice

First presented by Eva Productions at the Upstairs at the Landor Theatre in 1996, it is set in a British Rail café on a Sunday night.

There are two girls working at the counter, STEPH and Laura. STEPH is married with a boy, Tom, to bring up and looks forward to coming out in the evening. Laura is younger and anxious to move on. Throughout the action they carry out their work routine, stopping only to take on the characters of the various customers that come into the café for a coffee and a bit of a chat.

In this scene STEPH is going from table to table filling up pepper and salt pots, while Laura is unpacking bread and moaning about the job and the 'weirdos' they meet. STEPH laughs to herself. She loves the 'weirdos' and likes working in the café.

Published by First Writes Publications, London

STEPH

I call them pieces of pie . . . your weirdos. I love them! All little bits of pie, making up one great big pie! *(She laughs to herself.)* . . . I like it here, all the comings and goings. Makes me feel central with everyone else around me. *(Pause.)* I came into this station you know, when we moved down here. I was a comer and goer . . . a piece of pie! Except I only came and I haven't gone yet. Funny I end up working here . . . it's funny that! . . . *(Pause)* Oh Laura, Friday . . . oh! – Tom had a fall at school, bumped his head! . . . I was so worried. It hurts you in here *(Tapping her heart.)* when they hurt themselves. It's worse than doing it yourself. I wasn't even there. . . . He's all right now. He had mild concussion though. . . . You know, when I was Tom's age at school, I wanted to be the angel Gabriel in the Nativity, but I were never allowed! I had to be a shepherd and stuff a cuddly toy under me arm and pretend it were a lamb! Oh, but I wanted to be that angel! Wear a big white sheet and a bit of tinsel in your hair! You know, the angel got all the attention and the shepherds were just left milling around. I bumped my head one year and they didn't notice, till I fell over and knocked Mary off her cuddly donkey and she started crying and I got the blame! I wasn't allowed to be a shepherd again the next year. They said I wasn't meek and humble enough! So they made me be Joseph, cos I were the tallest in class. I hope my Tom gets to play Gabriel . . . but if he takes after me he'll get stuck at the back somewhere . . . Strange I remember all that. Sticks in your mind, don't it?

AMIE
early 20s

A JOVIAL CREW
Richard Brome
Adapted by Stephen Jeffreys

First presented in 1641, *A Jovial Crew* was the last play to be performed before the outbreak of the English Civil War. This adaptation was presented by the Royal Shakespeare Company at the Swan Theatre, Stratford-upon-Avon in 1992.

The two daughters of wealthy landowner, Squire Oldrents, have run off with a crew of beggars, and are joined by their lovers and the house steward, Springlove. They all look forward to a life of carefree abandon. AMIE is the ward of Justice Clack, a local magistrate. She is betrothed to young Tallboy, but runs away with her father's clerk, Martin, to escape a loveless marriage. The couple meet up with Springlove and the crew of beggars and AMIE decides to join them.

In this scene, she runs in breathless, followed by Martin, and flings herself down on the ground laughing. She is beginning to tire of Martin and finds herself very much attracted to Springlove.

Published by Josef Weinberger Plays, London

AMIE

I have never known such running! My ankles are more scratches than skin, my feet are thorns and blisters and my garments torn into such beggar-state that I need no disguise! . . . My heart is knocking at my ribs like a hungry visitor at the door! This fellow Springlove - Oh an excellent fellow, is't not? And a sure and safe guide through hedge-holes and bramble tracks - . . . We are now (thanks to his good offices) safe from our pursuers . . . Good Martin, hold your tongue and do not hasten so to play the ingrate. Now, I am taken with a raging thirst from all this up and down scambling. There is a farmhouse over yonder, and, if you lov'd me, you would hasten there and beg a jug of water - . . . You err too much o' the side of caution. Go and do my bidding, or I will never under God's sun abide the ceremony you would have me undergo. . . . Go to't and fetch me water quick, before you are betrothed to a wrinkled corpse.

(Martin *goes,* AMIE *sits up.*)

I have not had such a frolic since I was a girl and played at touch and scurry with the village children. What a day is this: first to wake in a ditch with the open sky my canopy; then to run hungry into such good company; and last to play the cunning fox o'er hedge and ditch with half the huntsmen in the county at my back. And yet I am in woeful straits. This Springlove's a proper man - and yet perhaps he only seems so. I have made myself desperate running from a despis'd match to one I like but little better and now I am perplex'd. But peace, here he comes. Lie down heart and find a temperate rhythm for your dance.

EVELYN
50s

KINDERTRANSPORT
Diane Samuels

First produced by the Soho Theatre Company at the Cockpit Theatre, London in 1993 and at the Vaudeville Theatre in 1996.

Between 1938 and 1939 nearly ten thousand children, mostly Jews, were sent from Germany to Britain. One of these children, Eva Schlesinger, arrives in Manchester expecting her parents to join her later. When her parents fail to escape the Holocaust she changes her name to EVELYN and begins the process of denying her roots. EVELYN is now in her fifties. Her daughter, Faith, who is about to move into a flat of her own, believes her mother to be an ordinary middle-class English woman, until searching through the attic she comes across letters and photographs belonging to 'Eva'. She questions her grandmother who finally admits that 'Eva' and EVELYN are one and the same person. Faith is angry and hurt and quarrels bitterly with EVELYN.

In this scene EVELYN is tearing up papers in the attic, trying to remove every trace of her past. Faith confronts her again, demanding that EVELYN tells her everything about her childhood in Germany and in particular, her parents.

Published by Nick Hern Books, London

EVELYN

Do you still want to know about my childhood, about my origins, about my parents? . . . Well, let me tell you. Let me tell you what little remains in my brain. And if I do, will you leave me alone afterwards. Will you please leave me alone? . . .

My father was called Werner Schlesinger. My mother was called Helga. They lived in Hamburg. They were Jews. I was an only child. I think I must have loved them a lot at one time. One forgets what these things feel like. Other feelings displace the original ones. I remember a huge cone of sweets that I had on my first day of school. There were a lot of toffees.

(She goes blank for a moment.)

I remember lots of books. Rows and rows . . . a whole house built of books and some of them were mine. A storybook filled with terrifying pictures . . . children's fingers being cut off, children whose teeth fall out and choke them while they're asleep, children being burnt in attic rooms and no one hearing them scream . . . Flames. Little flames flickering in a holder with lots of arms. Silver arms and one twisted, rocking leg holding them up. Old and faded. Rubbed away in patches. Wobbly candles which wouldn't stand straight, sticking out at strange angles. And one time . . . only once . . . being allowed to light them. Even striking the match myself. Just one, single time. And keeping watch while they melted to nothing in case they burned the house down . . . which would have been my fault because I lit them. The candles were all different colours. The little lights were the most beautiful . . . Silly lights . . . Silly, silly lights . . . . . .

The only other thing is a boy with a squint on the train I came away on. I kept trying not to look at him. Please believe me, Faith, there is nothing else in my memory from that time. It honestly is blank.

An excerpt (abridged) from *Kindertransport* by Diane Samuels.
Published by Nick Hern Books, The Glasshouse,
49a Goldhawk Road, London W12 8QP.

MISS SHEPHERD
late 70s

THE LADY IN THE VAN
Alan Bennett

First performed at the Queen's Theatre in 1999 and adapted by the author from his autobiographical memoirs, it is the story of Miss Mary Shepherd whom Alan Bennett first came across when she was living in a van parked in the street near his London home. Taking refuge with her van in his garden, originally for three months, she ended up staying for fifteen years.

MISS SHEPHERD is now seventy-eight and not at all well. Social Services have arranged for her to be taken to a day centre, and from there to be sent on to either a council home or hospital.

In this scene she has left the day centre of her own accord and is back again in the van in Alan Bennett's garden. Alan has brought her some flowers.

Published by Faber & Faber, London

MISS SHEPHERD

I've got a Horlicks jar they'll go in. There's some old Horlicks in it still but it won't do them any harm. Here. If you want water there's generally some collects in the dustbin lid.

Not been given flowers. There were always flowers. Flowers were routine. And I'd smile and curtsy. There was a piano at the day centre. *(She says this as if she has just been talking about the piano, as in a way she has.)* I didn't try and play it. I don't know that my fingers will run to it now. They had the wireless on all the time. Music. How are people supposed to avoid it?

[A. BENNETT: Do you want to avoid it?]

(vehemently) The soul in question was instructed to avoid it. Directions were given, sacrifices made, possibly. It was my mother I got it from. She was keenly ardent in her appreciation of classical music. I was just a girl, though older than my years in point of knowledge known and seeings of the spirit. Only I had it at my fingertips. I had it in my bones. Look. *(She shows her hands.)* It's not what it looks like, the piano. To the uninitiated the notes look the same. To me, no. Different, all of them. I could tell them in the dark. I could play in the dark, had to sometimes, possibly. And the keys were like rooms. C Major. D Minor. Dark rooms. Light rooms, going up or down a step into another room. It was a mansion to me, music. Heard in the spirit, possibly.

(Pause.)

Only it worried me that playing came easier to me than praying. And I said that, which may have been an error.

[A. BENNETT: Said it to whom?]

To an ordained priest of great reverence. My confessor. I loved my frocks. Long white arms. People clapping. The flowers brought on. He said that was another vent the devil could creep through. I asked, was there a middle way? Before I sat down at the keyboard I could possibly say, 'I dedicate this performance to God.' Or any saint my confessor might choose to nominate. Because it was God-given, I knew that. He said God-given was easily mistaken for devil-sent. So he outlawed the piano. Put paid to music generally. Said that dividends would accrue in terms of growth of the spirit. Which they did. They did. They did. I was good enough to be on the wireless. Earn a living. Offer it to God, Mary. Offer it to God. Cortot. Alfred Cortot. Have you heard of him?

[A. BENNET: He was famous.]

Yes. He was my teacher.

WENDY
London
late 30s

LIFE IS SWEET
Mike Leigh

First shown at the London Film Festival in 1990, it is described as a comedy in which the pain of family life is borne with a wry smile.

The family consists of WENDY and Andy and their twin daughters, Natalie, who works as a plumber, and Nicola, who is bulimic and doesn't work at all. Although at first WENDY seems rather silly, with her baby-talk of 'cheesie toasties', she is a woman of indomitable spirit and a caring wife and mother. And when Andy buys a rusty old caravan to start up a mobile snack bar selling burgers she stands by him.

In this scene WENDY is taking a group of about twenty-five little girls for a Saturday morning dancing class. She is more concerned with getting the girls to enjoy themselves than with anything formal or rigorous.

Published by Faber & Faber, London

WENDY

All right, Suzie . . . are you ready? Just move a little bit that way, darlin'.
That's it. OK, after four . . . One, two, three, four! Stretch! Yeah! Round
. . . stretch! That's a good girl, Lucy! One, two, three, stretch! One,
two, three . . . One, two, three, four! Round, smile! One, two, three .
. . and one, two, and cha-cha-cha! One, two, and cha-cha-cha! Very
good . . . doing well. And again – one, two, three, stretch, one, two,
three, four! Get your legs up! That's better! Stretch, right up! Like
you're stretching for sweets on the top shelf! Cha-cha-cha! One, two,
and cha-cha-cha! Very good . . . come on! One, two . . . Woo!! Come
on, enjoy yourselves!

(WENDY *now leads the* girls *round the hall in an informal
circle.*)

Right, put your hands on your hips, like that. Yeah, that's it. And the
other one! Now wave with both hands! Right? That's it. Very good –
come on, Laura, you can be leader now. Right out here . . . keep to
the edges – that's right! Let's have a bit of a bum-swing from you!
Above your heads – come on, hands up! Oh, swing those bums! That's
it. And you're doing that cleaning your mum's windows. *(Circular
hand motion.)* All right? And then you see your best friend . . . so
you're shoutin' out, 'Hi! It's me! I'm here!' *(Waving with both hands.)*
Say, 'Hi!' [GIRLS: Hi!]
Hi! [GIRLS: Hi!]
Say, 'It's me!' [GIRLS: It's me!]
'I'm here!' [GIRLS: I'm here!]
'Gimme a five-pound note!' [GIRLS: Give me a five-pound note!]
'I wanna go and spend it on sweets!' I thought that'd get you smilin'!
Thought you'd like that! Come on, 'oo's goin'a be the leader now,
then?

(WENDY *walks over to the girls' coats and things, which are
hanging on rows of hooks.*)

Right – come on, then . . . time to go home! Not too much of a rush
now – I don't want you trippin' over! *(The girls crowd round and
collect their belongings.)* Right, get your coats and shoes on outside,
as usual. All right, d'you wanna put your little cardigan on, Suzie? Eh?
Put it on, 'cos you might get a little chill. Got your sleeves inside out
– get your coats, now! If you can't reach your bags, I'll get them
down! 'T's it, put your cardie on – hope your headache's better soon!
(WENDY *helps Suzie on with her cardigan.*) . . . All right? 'Bye,
darlin' – bye! . . . Your bag's next door? All right, don't worry. 'Oo's is
the green coat? *(She holds up the green coat.)*

RUTH
American
30

MADAME MELVILLE
Richard Nelson

First performed at the Vaudeville Theatre, London in October 2000, it is set in Paris in 1966.

Madame Melville is the story of Carl, a fifteen year old American boy and his brief affair with his literature teacher, the beautiful Claudie Melville.

Carl has spent the night at Madame Melville's apartment, having missed the last train home. The next morning Madame Melville's neighbour, RUTH calls round to see her. She is dressed in messy clothes with her hair uncombed and no makeup. She can't wait to talk about her new lover, Robert – the first Frenchman she has found interesting.

Published by Faber & Faber, London

RUTH
Robert says I should get a bigger bed. *(Then getting 'into' herself and her problems.)* This from a man who says he normally sleeps on the floor – or on one of those thinny thin mattresses from the orient? What are they called? He gets into my bed – but he is a big guy. How tall do you think Robert is? . . . Guess. . . . Something like that. We didn't wake you? I mean – he did play me two of his songs at something like four in the morning. I'm saying – Robert, sh-sh, sing in the morning. He says – *(French accent.)* 'I sing when I feel like singing.'
  (Beat.)
I've never seen a naked man strum a guitar before – you know: bouncing. It's an unnatural sight. He's got a cousin who has offered him a job. *(More random memories.)* And an uncle who's somehow in the government. They don't speak. He's been to America twice. Once to Florida with his parents when he was a boy. Then once to Manhattan where he bummed around for about three weeks, living off people he just met, sleeping – wherever. Once he slept under someone's sink that had a drip. In the middle of the night, he said, they turned on a light and there he was trying to fix the drip. He's very handy. You know my record-player that's been broken for weeks? He almost got it to work. That's what he said – he almost fixed it. *(She seems lost in a thought for a moment, then, changing gears, to Claudie.)* He's really young. *(To Carl.)* Where in America are you from?

MANON
young

MANON/SANDRA
Michael Tremblay
Translated by John Van Burek

First performed in Great Britain at the Traverse Theatre, Edinburgh
in 1984 and later transferred to the Donmar Warehouse, London.

The action crosscuts scenes from the life of a saintly girl, MANON,
obsessed by her religion, with those of Sandra, a sex-obsessed trans-
vestite. Both characters live on the Rue Fabre. Towards the end of
the play Sandra reveals that 'she' was MANON's childhood friend of
twenty years ago.

In this opening scene, MANON is sitting in her kitchen, rocking.
She is dressed all in black. Sandra, all in white, is sitting in her 'dress-
ing-room' doing her nails. MANON has bought herself a new rosary
that morning.

Published by Faber & Faber, London

MANON
I bought myself a new rosary this morning . . . It's beautiful. It's splen-
did! It cost me a lot of money, but I don't care, nothing's too beautiful
for God.
   (*Silence.*)
I don't know if I'll say it before Sunday though. It's awful . . . I'm
caught between two fires and I don't know what to do . . . If I say it
now, it won't count, because it hasn't been blessed yet and it would
be like I wasn't praying at all . . . but on the other hand, it's so beautiful . . . and so heavy. I bought it 'cause it was heavy. I'm sick of cheap
little rosaries that weigh nothing and look like nothing. I don't feel I'm
praying any more when I've got one in my hands . . . But this one . . .
When I saw this one, I was speechless. I was looking for a big rosary,
OK, but that big! When I saw it, I thought to myself: 'I don't believe it,
is that a real rosary or an ad for one?' . . . I was at the Oratory, because
they have the best selection . . . and the most beautiful. So, I asked the

lady if the big rosary was for sale. 'Why, of course,' she answered, 'and I'm telling you, it works wonders' . . . I took the rosary down myself while the lady went for the shopping bag.

(*Silence.*)

It's not plastic. No. Plastic's light as a feather. I don't know what it's made of. It's transparent, but it's very heavy. I can't figure it out.

(*Silence.*)

Maybe it's God's presence that's so heavy.

(*Silence.*)

. . .The lady was amazed when I told her I'd pay cash. Her eyes as big as saucers, she said: 'Aren't you afraid to walk around with all that money in your purse?' 'Oh, no,' I said, 'my Guardian Angel is with me and God's armed him like a soldier to protect me from wicked people.' Boy, did she laugh. I always make people laugh with my comparisons. I picked up my big package and caught my two buses home. A little boy on the 129 thought it was a set of blocks. But his mother told him: 'Why no, Raymond, can't you see, it's a big rosary. Look at the nice wooden crucifix, isn't that lovely?' Then she asked me: 'Is it for a church, Sister?' I went all red. It's not the first time that I've been mistaken for a nun, but it's the first time someone thought that I was carrying things for the Church! 'No,' I told her, 'it's for me. It's my rosary.' And with that, the lady starts laughing like a maniac. 'For the love of God,' she says, between a couple of hiccoughs, 'what're you gonna do with it, skip rope?' Well, I wasn't gonna stand for that! 'I'll have you know, lady, rosaries like this are made for people like you!', I screamed at her, right there on the bus, 'for people with near-sighted souls!' That shut her up. But she didn't look like she understood. People can be so thick when they decide that they want to be stupid. Well, too bad for her! I didn't even tell her I wasn't a nun!

(*Silence.*)

But still, that doesn't solve my problem. I must admit, I'm a little embarrassed to show up at the parish house with my shopping bag to get it blessed. I should have had it blessed when I bought it, but I was too excited. I was too anxious to see how it would look in the place where I wanted to put it. No, I'll wait until it's blessed before I start praying on it. It's a sacrifice. I'll offer to God for the sins of that crazy lady who understood nothing and who laughed at me on the bus. I'll pray for her on my little rosaries and wait to pray for myself on the big one.

An excerpt (abridged) from *Manon/Sandra* by Michel Tremblay, translated by John Van Burek. Published by Nick Hern Books, The Glasshouse, 49a Goldhawk Road, London W12 8QP.

BERENICE
Black American
45

THE MEMBER OF THE WEDDING
Carson McCullers

First produced in New York in 1950 at the Empire Theater and revived in the States in the 1990s, it is set in a small southern town in America in 1945.

Frankie, a dreamy, restless girl adores her brother Jarvis and his fiancee Janice, and has made up her mind that after their wedding she will go with them and they will all three travel the world together. She confides these dreams to BERENICE the cook.

In this scene BERENICE is in the kitchen cooking, with little John Henry from next door sitting on a stool beside her. Frankie has been missing all day and now she comes in, having bought a special dress for the wedding and carrying a suitcase which she intends to pack in preparation for leaving with Jarvis and Janice after the ceremony. She tells BERENICE that while she was in town she caught a glimpse of something out of the corner of her eye – a double shape – and suddenly in her mind her brother and his bride were standing there, and then when she turned and looked it was only two coloured boys. BERENICE remembers having the same sort of feeling herself, the year after her beloved husband, Ludie died.

Published by New Directions, New York

BERENICE
It was the April of the following year that I went one Sunday to the church where the congregation was strange to me. I had my forehead down on the top of the pew in front of me, and my eyes were open – not peeping around in secret, mind you, but just open. When suddenly this shiver ran all the way through me. I had caught sight of something from the corner of my eye. And I looked slowly to the left. There on the pew, just six inches from my eyes, was this *thumb*. . . . Now I have to tell you. There was only one small portion of Ludie Freeman which was not pretty. Every other part about him was

handsome and pretty as anyone would wish. All except this right thumb. This one thumb had a mashed, chewed appearance that was not pretty. You understand. . . . And as I knelt there just staring at this thumb, I begun to pray in earnest. I prayed out loud! Lord, manifest! Lord, manifest! . . . Manifest, my foot! *(Spitting.)* You know who that thumb belonged to? . . . Why, Jamie Beale. That big old no-good Jamie Beale. It was the first time I ever laid eyes on him. . . . I guess I felt drawn to him on account of that thumb. And then one thing led to another. First thing I know I had married him. . . .

And the very same thing occurred in the case of Henry Johnson. . . . No. It was not the thumb this time. It was the coat. *(Frankie and John Henry look at each other in amazement. After a pause Berenice continues.)* Now when Ludie died, them policy people cheated me out of fifty dollars so I pawned everything I could lay hands on, and I sold my coat and Ludie's coat. Because I couldn't let Ludie be put away cheap. . . . It was walking down the street one evening when I suddenly seen this shape appear before me. Now the shape of this boy ahead of me was so similar to Ludie through the shoulders and the back of the head that I almost dropped dead there on the sidewalk. I followed and run behind him. It was Henry Johnson. Since he lived in the country and didn't come into town, he had chanced to buy Ludie's coat and from the back view it looked like he was Ludie's ghost or Ludie's twin. But how I married him I don't exactly know, for, to begin with, it was clear that he did not have his share of sense. But you let a boy hang around and you get fond of him. Anyway, that's how I married Henry Johnson. . . .

Why, Frankie, don't you see what I was doing? I loved Ludie and he was the first man I loved. Therefore I had to go and copy myself forever afterward. What I did was to marry off little pieces of Ludie whenever I come across them. It was just my misfortune they all turned out to be the wrong pieces. My intention was to repeat me and Ludie. Now don't you see? . . . You don't! Then I'll tell you. You and that wedding tomorrow. That is what I am warning about. . . . I see what you have in mind. Don't think I don't. You see something unheard of tomorrow, and you right in the center. You think you going to march to the preacher right in between your brother and the bride. You think you going to break into that wedding, and then Jesus knows what else. . . . But what I'm warning is this. If you start out falling in love with some unheard-of thing like that, what is going to happen to you? If you take a mania like this, it won't be the last time and of that you can be sure. So what will become of you? Will you be trying to break into weddings the rest of your days?

ALLIE
young

MULES
Winsome Pinnock

Commissioned by Clean Break Theatre Company and first performed at the Royal Court Theatre Upstairs in 1996.

Girls are needed to traffic drugs. Preferably young girls who need cash and enjoy international travel. Risks include violence, betrayal, imprisonment, even death. Bridie works in the London Office. Her job is to recruit the girls. Lou and Lyla were picked up in a bar in Kingston, Jamaica, ALLIE in a London street.

In this scene ALLIE is with Bridie in a London hotel. She has just completed her first assignment. As she speaks she removes small packets of coke from her person. She takes off a wig she wears in which drugs have been secreted and peels wide strips of plaster from her legs and waist, under which again there are more packets of drugs. She talks excitedly.

Published by Faber & Faber, London

ALLIE

All through the flight I wanted to scratch my head, but I didn't want to draw attention to my hair. Besides, what if I scratched my head and the wig moved then everybody would have known I was wearing a wig, wouldn't they? They might get suspicious. So I had to put up with this itch. It drove me mad. I tried everything: I tried to ignore it, but the more you try to ignore something the more you think about it, don't you? So the itch is starting to get worse and worse and I'm trying to find ways to get rid of it without actually touching it. I try to go to sleep but the itch won't let me. I try to get myself so drunk that I'll fade away in an alcoholic blur, but the drink and the flight simply stimulate me and the itch is getting more ticklish. To make matters worse, I develop an itch on my stomach, so now I'm getting itchy all over and I can't do anything about it because I don't want to make the air hostesses suspect anything, and I can't go to the loo as this enormous bloke in the seat beside me has fallen asleep and I don't want to wake him up. . . . So I just had to exercise self-control and grin and bear it. . . . I wanted to scratch myself raw, but soon as I got out of the airport, the itch just disappeared. . . . Going through customs was another matter altogether. My heart was thumping. I could swear that everybody was staring at me. I noticed this man at customs looking at me. Should I look back at him, should I drop my gaze or should I smile? . . . Then, somehow, I don't know how, it was like somebody else took over. This really cool woman who had no nerves. My heart stopped beating, there was this silence inside me. I felt full of this power and I just walked past customs as though I expected to be allowed straight through. And I was.

SANDRA
London
mid-20s

MURMURING JUDGES
David Hare

First performed in the Olivier Theatre at the Royal National Theatre, London in 1991 and revived as part of the David Hare trilogy in 1993. The title of the play is from a legal expression meaning 'to speak ill of the judiciary', which is still an offence in Scottish Law.

The play centres around a young lawyer's first case and takes us through the criminal justice system – involving the police, the courts and the prisons – a system which is cracking at the seams. SANDRA BINGHAM is a young WPC. She is in uniform, small and neat with dyed-blond hair.

This scene takes place in the charge room of a large Inner-London police station, dominated by a long desk. There is activity going on behind her as she speaks directly to the audience.

Published by Faber & Faber, London

SANDRA
You see, it's all mess. That's what it is, mostly. If you take the charge room for instance, there's maybe thirty or forty people arrested in a day. Most of them are people who simply can't cope. They've been arrested before – petty thieving, deception, stealing car radios, selling stolen credit cards in pubs. Or not even that. Disturbing the peace. Failing to appear on a summons. Failing to carry out conditions of bail. Failing to produce a current car licence. Failing to fulfil Community Service. Getting drunk. Getting drunk and going for a joyride. Getting drunk and then driving home. Attacking your wife. Who then won't testify. Trying to cash a stolen cheque, only being so stupid you don't even try to make the signatures match. Opening telephone boxes. Fifty-fifty fights in clubs which are nobody's fault. Crimes of opportunity. Not being able to resist it. Then going back, thinking I got away with it last time. Possession. One acid tab. One Ninja Turtle sticker containing LSD. One smoke. One sniff. One toke. One three-quid packet. *(She smiles.)* That's the basic stuff. It's the stuff of policing. All you have to do with it is be a ledger clerk. You fill in bits of paper. Every officer carries thirty-six bits of paper about their person at any one time.

   (SANDRA *starts to move round the room to collect the boy
   she has just arrested. She stops a moment.*)
Policing's largely the fine art of getting through biros. And keeping yourself ready for the interesting bits.

LADY ONOLA
African
middle-aged

OROONOKO
Aphra Behn
A new adaptation by 'Biyi Bandele

This new adaptation of Aphra Behn's novella was first performed by the Royal Shakespeare Company at The Other Place, Stratford-upon-Avon in 1999.

It tells the story of a young African Prince, Oroonoko, who is tricked into slavery, separated from his love, the Princess Imoinda and transported to the British Colony of Surinam in South America, where he is persuaded to lead a slave revolt.

In this early scene, set in the King's palace in Coramantien, Oroonoko has just arrived back from the war. He asks for an audience with the King, his Grandfather, but Oromba, the King's Chief Adviser tells him that there is nothing he can do for him as His Highness is 'attending to eminently urgent affairs of the state'. At that moment the LADY ONOLA, a middle-aged courtesan enters. She is the outspoken ex-mistress of the King and is allowed to remain at court as she is the one person who is not afraid to tell His Highness – or anyone else – the truth.

Published by Amber Line Press, Charlbury, Oxfordshire

ONOLA
Affairs of the state? Did you say
Affairs of the state?
(*To* Oroonoko.) What Chief Orombo means is that His
Highness our dear King is keeping
His visitors waiting while he attempts
To insert his Royal Privilege
Into the comely virtues of a young maiden.
Much ado - dare I say - over nothing.
Were the King's penis a warrior - he
Wishes it were - it would have been beheaded
Long ago for persistent dereliction of duty. . . .
It is well known in the seraglio
That though the King never can
Sleep, his penis is forever nodding off. . . .
Your wives may have slept with a snake,
Chief Orombo, but not with the one
Between the King's legs. It is a worm
Bereft of limb, flattered into thinking
Itself a reptile. . . .
I did tell your second wife, Kemi, when she said
She was marrying you that you had not
Done badly by her, for she is beautiful and
So is her smile. You bedecked her with gold and bales
Of cloth. But I could see, from looking at you,
That you could not satisfy her in bed. What
She needed in bed - I told her - was a man who once he
Mounted her would not let off until the roof fell
Through. Not a glorified pimp who farms out
His wives and children to curry royal favour.

GABRIELLA PECS
30s

PENTECOST
David Edgar

First performed at The Other Place, Stratford-upon-Avon in 1994 and in London at the Young Vic in 1995. Described as the first serious response in the British theatre to the tragedy of Sarajevo and a political parable, this play takes place in an unnamed South-Eastern European country.

GABRIELLA PECS, art curator of the National Museum, has discovered a partly exposed painting on the wall of an abandoned church. The painting is similar to that of Giotto's *Lamentation* in the Arena Chapel, Padua and could be not only of great value, but might possibly change the history of Western art. GABRIELLA wants to remove the painting to the museum for safe-keeping and English art historian, Oliver Davenport agrees to help her. Their activities are questioned first by the Minister for Conservation of National Monuments and then by American art historian, Leo Katz who has been brought in as an expert witness. Eventually they are ordered to abandon their work, but before they can leave the church they are taken hostage by a group of refugees who demand citizenship and work permits in exchange for their release.

In this early scene GABRIELLA explains to Anna Jedlikova, the presiding Magistrate called in by Oliver, why it is imperative to remove the painting at this time. She is working from notes handed to her by Oliver; she is nervous but determined.

Note: The language of the 'country' used in the play is Bulgarian – although the country is not Bulgaria.

Published by Nick Hern Books, London

GABRIELLA
Um – Respected magistrate. We drag you here today for two – three reasons. First to show how this procedure to transfer painting – which you may hear accused to be a yanking off or ripping off or skinning off or flaying – is actually technique developed in middle ages and used to great effect for all time since. . . .

(She looks at Leo, *challengingly.)*

However, we also want show you *reason* for transferral. For though painting has survive so many century of candle-grease and sprinkling of holy water, shaking cause by bells – . . . What may be it cannot endure so well is to end up half way from zinc smelting works to major international autoroute. Particularly as painting faces back on autoroute and has one layer of brick remove. . . .

(Slight pause. GABRIELLA *is alarmed by* Leo's *silence but decides to plough gamely on.)*

So, question obviously remain as to why this painting matter. It unheard of. Anonymous. As you see from photo, not in excellent condition. But there is quite enough to tell that very similar to fresco of Italian master Giotto, painted in thirteen hundred five. With main difference that lady from behind is rock, and St John instead of throwing arm back in gesture of despair, leans one arm forward as if to comfort Virgin in her grief. And this is naturally all kind of error you must make if you are drawing from a drawing, or else out of memory.

(Leo recognises the quotation from his own remark.)

Except. Except we think that it is not this look like Giotto but that Giotto look like this. And if we are right, then it – fountainhead of next 600 years. To coin phrase, starting shot of great race to change Europe out from state of childish mediaeval superstition into modern rational universal man.

(Slight pause.)

And you know such progress can seem less big deal, if you go through your renaissance and enlightenment, if you have your Michelangelo and Mozart and Voltaire. Maybe if you reach to journey's end then it bit more easy to say, actually, this being grown up maybe not so hunkydory after all. But, for us, it is maybe bit different. For us, being child not so far back. For those who stand on Europe's battlements since all of last 600 years.

(Pause.)

And yes it probably was painted here by foreigner. But maybe too you understand what it is meaning to us if despite all Turkish occupation, despite Mongol yoke, still this painting made, and wanted, asked for, and appreciated here. Maybe then we may feel bit more universal, bit more grown up, maybe even bit more European.

An excerpt (abridged) from *Pentecost* by David Edgar.
Published by Nick Hern Books, The Glasshouse,
49a Goldhawk Road, London W12 8QP.

BARBS
Scots Glaswegian
39

PERFECT DAYS
Liz Lochhart

First performed at the Traverse Theatre, Edinburgh in 1998 and revived at the Hampstead Theatre, London in 1999.

BARBS MARSHALL is a celebrity hairdresser working in Glasgow. She has her own show on local television and lives in a trendy apartment that she has designed herself. She is successful, but it is not enough. She is separated from her husband who has found himself a new girlfriend, and is approaching her thirty-ninth birthday.

In this opening scene she has just finishing cutting her friend Alice's hair, as she describes in detail her latest romantic disaster.

Published by Nick Hern Books, London

BARBS

So, Alice, I was telling you, we get to Glasgow airport, guy on the desk recognises me, we get an upgrade, very nice, thank you very much, First Class practically empty, great, spread out a bit, relax, the champagne cocktails, the blue blue sky, the white fluffy clouds beneath us . . . I'm feeling: OK maybe he's not got the highest IQ in the world but he does have a gorgeous profile and at least he's not wearing that fucking awful jumper that he turned up in wan night, tucked into his trousers can you believe, and gave me a red neck in front of Brendan from work.

I mean true and everlasting love it is not, but he's a nice guy and all that, own teeth, daft about me, well so far, it's only been three or four weeks, defin-ately dead keen, or so I've been led to believe by the dinners, the phonecalls, the nipping my heid about Paris – how he used to live there how there are all these sweet wee dinky little special places he knows that he'd like to take me, so there we are, we get to the hotel and here they've overbooked so this time we get an automatic upgrade to the four star no problem, it's gorgeous, the corner room, the fruitbowl, the flowers, the complimentary choco-lates, the half bottle of champagne, the big kingsize bed all turned down at the corner . . . And – now, to let you know, Alice – back home in Glasgow I've been avoiding it, by the way, because truth to tell I do not really fancy him, at least I do not fancy him when I am actually *with* him, I've been, frankly, postponing the inevitable for this weekend where I have calculated, quite correctly according to my Predictor Kit, I will be *ovulating* – and he says to me he can't sleep with me because he's Met Someone and he's fallen in love! No, correction, he can *sleep* with me, but we can't have sex because that would be him being unfaithful to his new wee dolly inamorata.

I'm like: What? I'm like: What are we doing here? And Why? He's like: well, it's a fantastic city, and I'm his best friend – best friend! – and he wants to show me it and he didn't want to disappoint me!

An excerpt (abridged) from *Perfect Days* by Liz Lochhart.
Published by Nick Hern Books, The Glasshouse,
49a Goldhawk Road, London W12 8QP.

SARAH
30s

A PLACE AT THE TABLE
Simon Block

First performed at the Bush Theatre, London in February 2000.

The action takes place in the Board/Conference Room of a small television production company, where ideals and artistic integrity are quickly elbowed for success and 'a place at the table'. SARAH SLATER is a script editor. Her success depends on developing an idea for a new and 'very different' series to impress James, her Head of Department. She has discovered Adam, a young writer who has just had a play produced with a disabled character in the central role, but he is not prepared to sacrifice his ideals for a TV soap and has walked out on her. Five months later he returns, having completed six whole episodes, based on his play – but it is too late. A new comedy series is in the pipeline. He accuses SARAH of using people to further her own career.

In this scene SARAH explains that she can no longer support lost causes. She was even unable to help her friend, Kate, when she lost her job and was escorted out of the building.

Published by Nick Hern Books, London

SARAH

Since we last met a lot of comedy water has flowed under a lot of comedy bridges, Adam. . . . Look. When Kate was walked out of this building five months ago she was begging me to help her. I wanted to say something. Call something comforting as she was escorted to the emergency stairwell. But a voice in my head said *'enough'*. *'Enough lost causes. Don't you dare move so much as a muscle'*. *(Beat.)* And then I returned to this room and found you'd gone too. *(Beat.)* That was more or less the final straw. . . . Having eluded it for so long I wanted to know what success at least *felt like* before I cleared my desk. If only someone else's. The crates of James' awards were over there. I remember unpacking them, and carefully lining them up on the carpet in a neat row. And as I moved along the row, reading the plaque on each - imagining my name in place of James' - I discovered . . . I discovered and *realised* at the same moment . . . . . . All the awards were for the same show. In my haste to genuflect before his prestige I had overlooked - no. I had *failed to register* the significance in the fact that he wasn't trailing a *string* of successes behind him. Only the *one*. But you land the big prize the little ones will surely follow. Topping a television festival in Germany. Winning a viewer's poll in Prague. Not a *repeated* success. Just one, and its echo. . . . The discovery made me realise James wasn't some media *sensation*. Merely flesh and blood running as far as his single stroke of luck would take him. So when I looked at James afresh, I understood it wasn't his success I coveted. But that *ease with himself* his success had engendered. And I understood that I needed to feel at ease with *my* self more than I needed to keep chasing the world with a match and gasoline. More than anything else, in fact. . . . They can call it what they like. They haven't been trying to be me for 36 years. *(Turns to the window and looks through the blind.)* *(Beat.)* From up here you can see half of London. Every house and flat. Every bedsit and maisonette. Every front room, lounge and kitchen. Every bedroom and study. Televisions in every one. *(Beat.)* From this window you can see half the television sets in London. *(Facing Adam.)* And if just half of those are tuned into our not especially good, but not altogether awful humourless comic on a regular basis - well - my name might finally take root somewhere. *(Beat.)* Is that such a terrible thing to want, Adam?

An excerpt (abridged) from *A Place at the Table* by Simon Block. Published by Nick Hern Books, The Glasshouse, 49a Goldhawk Road, London W12 8QP.

MRS BETTERTON
50s

PLAYHOUSE CREATURES
April De Angelis

First performed at the Haymarket Theatre Studio, Leicester in 1993 and later that year at the Lyric Studio, Hammersmith, it is set in Restoration London and follows the lives of four actresses, one of them the famous Nell Gwyn - all to some extent dependent on their rich protectors or 'keepers'.

MRS BETTERTON, leading lady of the company and wife of actor manager Thomas Betterton, has worked with her husband since their early days in the theatre together. Now she has been told she is too old to play leading parts anymore. Audiences want to see younger actresses in her roles and it is time for her to retire.

In this scene she is announcing her retirement to the other ladies in the company - Mrs Farley, Mrs Marshall, Nell Gwyn and Doll Common.

Published by Samuel French, London

MRS BETTERTON

From today I shall not be attending the theatre on a regular basis.
. . . Mr Betterton has talked to me. . . . Some younger actresses must
be given a chance. People like to see them. . . . They will partner Mr
Betterton. We were partners for many years. Many years. *(She sits
very still and does not move.)*
I used to work in the wardrobe. And I used to watch and watch and
wonder what it would be like. You know, to . . . do it. The acting. I
used to help my husband with his lines. And naturally, I learnt them
too. Then one day, he was playing Othello, and his Iago fell sick. He
ate something that disagreed with him. A pork pie. Anyway, it was
rotten. Mr Betterton was caught short and could not find anyone else
at such little notice to do the part. Except for me. I'd read it with
him many times. We knew it could mean trouble if the bishops found
me out, being a woman, but we were younger and reckless and
we thought no-one would ever know. . . . We got away with it. We
were very close, Mr Betterton and I, and it was as if I hung off his
breath, and he off mine, and the words flew between us. That was
my first time. *(Pause.)*
After that we did it on a regular basis. My fool to his Lear, his Falstaff
to my Hal. And then, of course, the day came when everything
changed and for the first time we women were permitted by Royal
decree to act upon a stage. A great stir it caused. And I was one of
the first ever and when I spoke, a great hush descended on the
house, and it was as if the men and women gathered there were
watching a miracle, like water turning to wine or a sick man coming
to health. *(Pause.)*
It was then I knew that I had done a terrible thing and that nothing
would ever be the same for me again. I had tasted a forbidden fruit
and its poisons had sunk deep into my soul. You see, Iago is like a
whip that drives the life around him, when Hal makes a choice the
whole world holds its breath. I never forgot that feeling. The poison's
still in my blood. Like a longing. A longing. I looked for that poison
everywhere and couldn't find it. Not in the Desdemonas or Ophelias.
Only in her, the dark woman. *(Pause.)*
We were partners for many years. And when he told me it was over,
I swear he had tears in his eyes. I had never seen him cry before,
except, of course, when the part required it.

PORTIA
Irish
30

PORTIA COUGHLAN
Marina Carr

This Abbey Theatre production was commissioned by the National Maternity Hospital in Dublin as part of its Centenary Celebrations. It was first performed at the Peacock Theatre, Dublin in 1996 and later that year at the Royal Court Theatre, London. The play is set in Ireland in the Belmont Valley in the Midlands in present time.

PORTIA COUGHLAN lives life in monstrous limbo, haunted by a yearning for her spectral twin brother, Gabriel, now lying at the bottom of the Belmont river. She is unable to find any love for her wealthy husband and children, seeking solace in soulless affairs, deeply afraid of what she might do next.

It is PORTIA's thirtieth birthday. At the beginning of this scene we see the spirit of her twin brother, Gabriel, as he wanders by the Belmont river singing. PORTIA is in her living room, leaning against the door, eyes closed and listening to the song. The doorbell rings but she ignores it. Her mother, Marianne, lets herself into the house. PORTIA's eyes are still closed as she speaks to her mother. The song gets fainter as Gabriel drifts off.

Published by Faber & Faber, London

PORTIA

Knew be tha witchy ring ud be yarself an' ya'd be bargin' in afore long acause ya never learnt, Mother, t'allow a person space an' quieh. . . .

[MARIANNE: An' wheer's yar children? Playin' 'roun' tha Belmont River ah suppose. You be luchy tha don' fall in an drown thimsilves wan a these days.]

Ya'd liche thah wouldn' ya, wapin' ah tha grave a' wan a' yar darlin' gran'sons. Be histora rapatin' udself, wouldn't ud now, be liche buryin' Gabriel all over agin. Ah knows how your bihher mine works, ya thinche thah if wan a' my sons was drownt thah mebbe ya could asplaine away how me twin was lost. Well mother, natin'll ever asplaine thah, natin'. . . . Ah rade subtext mother, words dropt be accident, phrases covered over, sintinces unfinished, an' ah know tha topography a' your mine as well as ah know ever' inch an' ditch an' drain a' Belmont Farm. So don't you bluster in here an' puh a death wish an my sons jus' acause ya couldn' save yar own. My sons'll be fine for if ah does natin' else ah lave thim alone an' no marche be behher than a blache wan. . . . He woulda bin thirty taday as well . . . sometimes ah thinche on'y half a' me is left, tha worst half . . . D'ya know thon'y rason ah married Raphael? Noh acause you an' Daddy says ah should, noh acause he war rich, ah chare natin' for money, naw thon'y rason I married Raphael was acause of hees name, a angel's name sem as Gabriel's, an' ah though' be osmosis or jus' pure wishin' thah wan'd tache an' tha qualihies a th'other. Buh Raphael is noh Gabriel an' never will be . . . An' ah dreamt abouh him agin las' nigh'. Was wan a' thim drames as is so rale ya thinche ud's actualla happenin'. Gabriel had chome ta dinner here an' ater he goh up ta lave an' ah says, 'Gabriel stay for tha weechind', an' Gabriel demurs ouha poliheness ta me an' Raphael. An' ah says, 'Gabriel, ud's me Portia, yar twin, don' be polihe, there's no nade wud me' . . . an' thin he turns an' smiles an' ah know he's gointa stay an' me heart blows open an stars falls ouha me chest as happens in drames . . . we war so aliche, warn't we mother? . . . Chem ouha tha womb howldin' hands . . . whin God war handin' ouh souls, he musta goh mine an' Gabriel's mixed up, aither thah or he gev us jus' tha wan atwane us an' ud wint inta tha Belmont River wud him . . . Oh Gabriel ya had no righ' ta discard me so, ta floah me an tha world as if ah war a ball a' flotsam, ya had no righ' . . . (Begins to weep uncontrollably.)

PAULA
London
young

THE POSITIVE HOUR
April De Angelis

First performed by Out of Joint at Hampstead Theatre, London in 1997.

Miranda is a social worker with no shortage of problems. Not the least of these is PAULA, an unemployed single mother who has taken up prostitution to survive and whose eight year old daughter, Victoria is in foster care.

The play opens in Miranda's office. It is her first day back at work after her 'nervous collapse'. She is confronted by a distraught PAULA, demanding that her daughter is returned to her immediately.

Published by Faber & Faber, London

PAULA

I don't want any more bollocks. . . . Bollocks. . . . I'm a desperate woman. You must've seen one of us before? We smoke and have hastily applied mascara. It's my daughter. Victoria Savage. Eight and three-quarters. Her favourite groups are Spice Girls and Michael Jackson. I haven't got the heart to tell her he's a pervert. I mean, children are in their own special world, aren't they? . . . Temporarily fostered with the Clements. Mr and Mrs Patrick of Sussex. They don't like me going there. They say it upsets Victoria. Course it does. I'm her mother. It's a wrench when I leave. She cries, I cry. It's a fucking mess. Patrick's a bank manager and Isobel doesn't know what to do with herself. They have a mug tree. Know the sort? Victoria's a very demanding child. That house was dead and now they're wetting themselves with having a bit of life in their life, but it's my fucking bit of life. . . . You see, this thing has happened in their heads. Somehow they think they are Victoria's parents and I am a passing annoyance. . . . And people are going to look at them and look at me and think she's better off with them. But she's my daughter. . . .

Do you like me? . . . Because it's important, isn't it, Miranda, that you like me? What you think is important? . . . So what are you going to do about Victoria? . . .

No one's listening to me. . . .

A process? . . . Five months now they've had her. . . . So how long's a process? . . . I'm sick of people keep putting me off. . . .

Don't fucking Paula me. (*She pulls a razor blade out of her bag and holds it to her wrist.*) Don't even fucking move. . . . I'm never happy, not without Victoria. I wake up in the morning and it's like there's a big hole in my chest only I'm too scared to look down because once I do I'm going to feel this pain. . . . No. Let's be hysterical. Let's have blood.

We must start the whole thing moving now. . . . Moving, that's good, Miranda.

LISA
London
17

THE POWER OF THE DOG
Ellen Dryden

First performed at The Orange Tree Theatre, Richmond in 1996.

Vivien Chadwick, Head of the English Department in a failing school run by an incompetent Headmaster, is preparing to take up a new appointment as Head of a school in South London. At the same time she is attempting to move house as well as visit her mother who has suffered a stroke. Added to these problems is LISA, a brilliant but difficult sixth-former, who she is encouraging to stay on at school and try for a place in university.

In this scene Vivien is in her study waiting for LISA to arrive for an extra tutorial. LISA turns up late as usual with the same old excuses – waiting thirty-five minutes for the bus and Mum being stroppy. Vivien asks if there is any chance of Mum coming to see her.

Published by First Writes Publications, London

LISA

Nah! She doesn't like schools. Give her panic attacks. *(Pause.)* And I don't want you to come to my house. . . .

> (LISA *turns her back. Then changes the subject with great energy.*)

Listen. I reckon you owe me ten quid. I went to see that Midsummer Night's Dream. It was crap! Helena was about thirty-five, kept chucking herself all over the place – tossing her hair back and flinging her arms about. You know – just like young people always do when we're in love. Nearly ruptured herself. She was about six inches shorter than Hermia as well, so she'd got these gross high heels and Hermia had to bend at the knees all through the quarrel scene. And the Mechanicals wandered about in the audience and talked to us. I hate that! And Peter Quince sat in the Stalls and shouted his lines from there. And the fairies all lived in cardboard boxes and had tattoos. Puck was a drug-pusher. And it went on for nearly four hours. I reckon ours was better. And I couldn't afford it! . . . Hey and guess what! Theseus and Hypolita played Oberon and Titania! Isn't that original? Everybody liked it except me. I wanted to get up and kill them all. Bunch of tossers. . . . It was everything you say was wrong – . . . I really love that play . . . I don't think this had any . . . respect. And it wasn't – magic . . .

> (*She stops, lost in thought for a moment.*)

I know. 'The best in this kind are but shadows and the worst no worse if imagination amend them . . . It must be your imagination then and not theirs.'

> (*She is very still. Her face becomes a mask.*)

(Very quietly.) I like – magic. *(Briskly.)* I suppose I'm talking rubbish – everybody else says it's brilliant. And they're paid to be in the imagination business, aren't they? And I've got no right to criticize them.

VIVIEN
40s

THE POWER OF THE DOG
Ellen Dryden

First performed at The Orange Tree Theatre, Richmond in 1996.

VIVIEN CHADWICK, Head of the English Department in a failing school run by an incompetent Headmaster, is preparing to take up a new appointment as Head of a school in South London. At the same time she is attempting to move house as well as visit her mother who has suffered a stroke. Adding to her problems is Lisa, a difficult but brilliant student, who has been coming to her for extra tutorials. A colleague, Richard Shaw, has called VIVIEN urgently at her mother's cottage to say that her study has been broken into and the contents vandalised. Everything points to Lisa, who is resentful because VIVIEN neglected to tell her she was leaving.

In this scene Richard is helping her to clear up the study. VIVIEN is hurt and angry, but determined not to report the matter.

Published by First Writes Publications, London

VIVIEN

(Biting her lip.) Yes all right. I am angry. I am – hurt. Let down. I'm feeling pretty petty . . . And it's all my fault, isn't it? I picked out a little – guttersnipe – and tried to change her life. Very presumptuous. Meddling, interfering, insensitive, boneheaded *do-gooder*. Using her to make me feel good. I've got what I deserve, haven't I? I suppose I expected her to know the rules – to behave like a nice, well-mannered, *(With loathing)* grateful little middle-class miss with just a few working-class rough edges that exposure to my superior culture could smooth away! It won't do her any good to be charged with criminal damage will it? *(With a little laugh of self disgust.)* She's pretty damaged already isn't she? . . . And I – have done my best to . . . damage her even further. And I don't want the humiliation. . . . End of experiment. Once I've cleared out of here I'll stick rigidly to the rules.

(She is rigid with tension.)

(With a sudden outburst.) I'm no sodding good at people, that's my trouble! I've got all the right ideas – wonderfully perceptive about characters in books – I don't miss a nuance! *(Brightly.)* I don't know why I'm making such a fuss. All teachers have their failures, don't they? I know why she did it but I wish she hadn't done it to me. But then that's only pride. I couldn't face Mrs Parker saying, 'I told you so!' So I'll just leave this room completely blank. Wiped clean. No trace of me – or anybody else. Let's face it, by half term everybody will have forgotten me. And if Lisa doesn't turn up everyone will breathe a collective sigh of relief. After all, it doesn't rate very high on the scale of atrocities, does it? Burning a few books. Not compared with knifings in the playground and drug-pushers at the gates. *(With a little laugh.)* I've been pushing the really dangerous drugs haven't I?

RITA
Welsh
20s

A PRAYER FOR WINGS
Sean Mathias

First presented at the Edinburgh Festival at the Scottish Centre in 1985 and later transferred to the Bush Theatre, London.

The action takes place in an old church that has been poorly converted into a dwelling on the outskirts of Swansea, where RITA lives with her invalid mother. Every day she has to wash, dress, shop, cook for her and help her in and out of her wheelchair. Unemployment is high and she can't get a job. Her only break in the monotony is touching up the boys down at the Labour for a few shillings and sometimes bringing them back to her upstairs bedroom to earn a bit more. She prays for a 'handsome man with real manners'. If she had wings she could fly away.

In this scene it is early morning. RITA is sitting up in bed and her mother is calling out to her.

Published by Amber Lane Press, Charlbury, Oxfordshire

RITA
I'm having extra five minutes.
  (*Pause.*)
All right?
  (*Pause.*)
That be all right?
  (*Silence.*)
(*Aside.*) Sod her, 'cos I am anyway. . . . To tell the truth, I don't feel like getting up at all today. I could quite happily lie here in bed all day long. Under the covers. What's there to get up for? Let's be honest, now. What is there? All she thinks about is her bleeding stomach. She's not like a woman with illness. She's like a woman on bleeding holiday. Oh, I wouldn't half mind a holiday myself. Never been on holiday. I'd travel far, I can tell you. Tell you where I'd go, well, where I'd like to go. I'd like to go to America. Land of sunshine

and something, isn't it? I'd go on the Q.E.2. To America. Have a big luxurious cabin. They'd be running round me. All them stewards. I'd have kippers in the morning and that fizzy wine with orange in. Champagne. That's it. I'd say, 'Bring me a magnum.' That'd keep me going. And I'd be lying there. Lying in peach satin. I'd have my hair all curly. My lifestyle would be very executive. That's the word, isn't it? Down the Job Centre you see that sometimes. Executive Posts. I bet you get a lot of trimmings in an executive post. And we'd sail into New York. And there'd be a big car to meet me. An executive car. Take me to some nice hotel. A hotel that had a door that went round and round. I've never been in one of them. I've only been up the escalators once. That was in the Co-op in Swansea. Mam says David Evans have got a lift. But we never went in there. Too dear, she says. Mind you, they got a lift down the D.H.S.S., but it stinks. Stinks of piss. I prefer the stairs myself. And a man would say, 'Let me take your luggage, madam.' I'd have twelve suitcases, 'cos I'd go to so many parties. Go out dancing. The cinema. I'd have a different frock for every film I saw. And people'd come to see me in my hotel room. A suite, isn't it? They calls it a suite. When it's in a hotel. Only suite I've seen was down the Co-op. Three piece suite, brown and beige. Mam fancied it. Contemplated H.P. I said, 'H.P.! We haven't got enough for bleeding rent.' And I'd have a big bed. Bigger than this, mind. A king size. Or maybe queen even. I'd lie on it all right. Towels by my side. Dry my locks. Oh, there's a trip I fancies, mind. There's a trip I'd go on. . . . I wonder if New York's bigger than Swansea. Big as Cardiff, maybe. Bet it is. Bet it's bigger than Sheffield, bigger than Manchester, Liverpool even. I bet it's bigger than Birmingham, Bangor, Llandudno, Aberystwyth, Brecon, Haverfordwest, Milford Haven, Builth Wells. Bigger than Neath, that's for sure. . . . Aye, waiter, we'll have two Dover sole. Send them up to my suite. With half a magnum.

LADY CATHERINE DE BOURGH
middle-aged

PRIDE AND PREJUDICE
Jane Austen
Adapted for stage by Sue Pomeroy

First performed at the Key Theatre, Peterborough by Good Company in September 1995, as part of a 28-week tour, finishing at the Theatre Royal, Bath in June 1996. It is set in Regency England in the Hertfordshire village of Longbourn.

When a single young man of good fortune comes to live in the neighbourhood, Mrs Bennet is determined that he shall marry one of her five daughters. Her eldest daughter, Jane, is now engaged to Mr Bingley and her youngest, Lydia, who, much to the family's distress eloped with the infamous Mr Wickham, has returned home a married woman. Elizabeth, the second eldest, having turned down a proposal from her cousin, Mr Collins has, unknown to her mother, rejected the wealthy Mr Darcy, who has declared his love for her.

LADY CATHERINE DE BOURGH is a wealthy dowager, a 'fine looking woman' according to Mrs Bennet, and an aunt to Mr Darcy. She represents the backbone of the English aristocracy, is steeped in tradition and believes she has a divine right to organise other people's lives, interfere with personal issues and maintain the purity of the Darcy family line. She is, in her own way, breaking the mould for she has inherited the de Bourgh family fortune and line, highly unusual for a woman at that time.

In this scene LADY CATHERINE arrives at the Bennet's house demanding to speak to Elizabeth. Mrs Bennet hastily retreats, taking her other daughters with her and leaving Elizabeth to face LADY CATHERINE alone.

LADY CATHERINE

I hope you are well, Miss Bennet. That person I suppose to be your mother. And that I suppose is one of your sisters. Miss Bennet, I should be pleased to talk to you alone on a private matter. . . . You can be at no loss to understand the reason of my journey hither. *(Lizzy is at a complete loss.)* . . . Miss Bennet, I am not to be trifled with. A report of a most alarming nature reached me two days ago. I was given to understand that not only was your elder sister on the point of being married most advantageously, but that you would soon afterwards be united to my own nephew, Mr Darcy. . . . I know it to be a scandalous falsehood, but I have nevertheless come to make my sentiments known to you. . . . You may pretend ignorance Miss Bennet but I insist on being satisfied. Has my nephew made an offer of marrage? I am his nearest relation and must know all his most intimate concerns. Your arts, in the course of some infatuation, may have made him forget his duty to himself and his family. *(Lizzy is giving nothing away.)* Let me be understood. This match can not take place. No, never. Mr Darcy is engaged to my daughter. They are intended. Whilst yet in their cradles we planned the union. Now, to be usurped by a young woman of inferior birth, and wholly unallied to the family! Mr Darcy is of the noblest lineage. Is he to be ruined by the upstart pretensions of some chancing young woman without name, connections or fortune? If you were mindful of your own good, you would not wish to quit that sphere to which you are accustomed! . . . Obstinate, headstrong girl – true you are a gentleman's daughter, but who was your mother? Who are your uncles and aunts? Miss Bennet, I am shocked and astonished. I was led to believe I would find a young woman of some reason and discernment. But do not delude yourself with the belief that I shall ever recede. I shall not leave this house until you have given me the answers I require. *(Lizzy attempts to walk out.)*

(Playing her final card.) Not so hasty if you please! I am no stranger to the details of your sister's infamous elopement. The whole county knows her marriage was a patched up business. And is such a woman to be the sister in law of my dear nephew! By heaven! Of what are you thinking? Are the shades of Pemberley to be thus polluted? . . . So, you refuse then to oblige me. You are determined to ruin him and expose him to the contempt of the world. This is your final resolve! Very well. I shall now know how to act. I take no leave of you Miss Bennet. I send no compliments to your mother. I am most seriously displeased. *(Exit.)*

MIA
Los Angeles
young

PULP FICTION
Quentin Tarantino

Pulp Fiction was awarded the Palme d'Or at the Cannes Film Festival in 1994. It is a trio of stories rotating around the violent misadventures of a collection of outlaws, right out of the pages of pulp fiction.

Jules is working for the infamous club owner, Marsellus Wallace. Marsellus is leaving for Florida and has asked Vincent to take care of his wife, MIA – a young actress who recently played the lead in an unsuccessful TV pilot.

In this scene Vincent and MIA are sitting at a table in Jackrabbit Slim's – a 1950s style diner. Vincent asks MIA about the television pilot and here she describes her fifteen minutes of fame.

Published by Faber & Faber, London

MIA

That was my fifteen minutes.... It was a show about a team of female secret agents called 'Fox Force Five.' ... 'Fox Force Five.' Fox, as in we're a bunch of foxy chicks. Force, as in we're a force to be reckoned with. Five, as in there's one ... two ... three ... four ... five of us. There was a blonde one, Sommerset O'Neal from that show 'Baton Rouge,' she was the leader. A Japanese one, a black one, a French one and a brunette one, me. We all had special skills. Sommerset had a photographic memory, the Japanese fox was a kung fu master, the black girl was a demolition expert, the French fox's speciality was sex ...... My speciality was knives. The character I played, Raven McCoy, her background was she was raised by circus performers. So she grew up doing a knife act. According to the show, she was the deadliest woman in the world with a knife. But because she grew up in a circus, she was also something of an acrobat. She could do illusions, she was a trapeze artist – when you're keeping the world safe from evil, you never know when being a trapeze artist's gonna come in handy. And she knew a zillion old jokes her grandfather, an old vaudevillian, taught her. If we woulda got picked up, they woulda worked in a gimmick where every episode I woulda told an old joke.... I only got the chance to say one, 'cause we only did one show ... No. It's really corny.... You won't like it and I'll be embarrassed.... I'm definitely not gonna tell ya, 'cause it's been built up too much.

(Buddy *comes back with the drinks.* MIA *wraps her lips around the straw of her shake.*)

Yummy! ...

(*Then the first uncomfortable silence happens.*)

Don't you hate that? ... Uncomfortable silences. Why do we feel it's necessary to talk about bullshit in order to be comfortable? ... That's when you know you found somebody special. When you can just shut the fuck up for a minute, and comfortably share silence....

Vincent! You still wanna hear my 'Fox Force Five' joke? ... You won't laugh because it's not funny. But if you still wanna hear it, I'll tell it. ... Okay. Three tomatoes are walking down the street, a poppa tomato, a momma tomato and a little baby tomato. The baby tomato is lagging behind the poppa and momma tomato. The poppa tomato gets mad, goes over to the baby tomato and stamps on him – (*Stamps.*) – and says: 'catch up.'

(*They both smile, but neither laughs.*)

See ya 'round, Vince.

LIZZIE
A Western State of America
27

THE RAINMAKER
N. Richard Nash

Produced at the St Martin's Theatre, London in 1956 and revived again in the States in the mid 1990s, *The Rainmaker* is set in a Western State of the USA on a summer day in a time of drought.

LIZZIE lives on a ranch with her father and two brothers, Jimmy and Noah. It is high time she was married, but no one has loved her or even found her beautiful. She has just returned from Sweetwater, where her father had sent her hoping she might make a match with one of her Uncle Ned's six boys. The family are anxious to know how she got on, and here she describes her disastrous visit.

Published by Samuel French, London

LIZZIE

Pop, let's not beat around the bush. I know why you sent me to Sweetriver. Because Uncle Ned's got six boys. Three of them are old enough to get married - and so am I. Well, I'm sorry you went to all that expense - the railroad ticket - all those new clothes - the trip didn't work. Noah, you can write it in the books - in red ink. . . .

(LIZZIE *kneels by her suitcase, opens it and tidies the garments in it.*)

The first three or four days I was there - I stayed in my room most of the time. . . . I knew what I was there for - and that whole family knew it, too. And I couldn't stand the way they were looking me over. So I'd go downstairs for my meals - and rush right back to my room. I packed - I unpacked - I washed my hair a dozen times - I read the Sears, Roebuck catalogue from cover to cover. And finally, I said to myself: 'Lizzie Curry, snap out of this.' Well, it was a Saturday night - and they were all going to a rodeo dance. So I got myself all decked out in my highest heels and my lowest cut dress. And I walked down to that supper table and all those boys looked at me as if I was stark naked. And then for the longest while there wasn't a sound at the table except for Uncle Ned slupping his soup. And then suddenly - like a gunshot - I heard Ned junior say: 'Lizzie, how much do you weigh?' . . . (LIZZIE *rises.*) I said, 'I weigh a hundred and nineteen pounds, my teeth are all my own and I stand seventeen hands high.' . . .

(LIZZIE *picks up the suitcase; wryly. She moves up L and puts the suitcase on the floor in the corner.*)

Then, about ten minutes later, little Pete came hurrying in to the supper table. He was carrying a geography book and he said: 'Hey, Pop - where's Madagascar?' Well, everybody ventured an opinion and they were all dead wrong. And suddenly I felt I had to make a good impression, and I said: 'It's an island in the India Ocean off the coast of Africa right opposite Mozambique.' . . . *(With a wail.)* Can I help it if I was good in geography? . . . Everything was so quiet it sounded like the end of the world. Then I heard Ned junior's voice: 'Lizzie you fixin' to be a schoolmarm?' . . .

(LIZZIE *moves to the hassock and sits on it.*)

And suddenly I felt like I was way back at the high school dance - and nobody dancing with me. And I had a sick feeling that I was wearing glasses again the way I used to. And I knew from that minute on that it was no go. So I didn't go to the rodeo dance with them - I stayed home and made up poems about what was on sale at Sears, Roebuck's.

ILSE
teenage

SPRING AWAKENING
Frank Wedekind
A new version by Ted Hughes

First performed in Germany in 1891 and in London at the Royal Court
Theatre in 1965. This new version by Ted Hughes was presented by
the Royal Shakespeare Company in The Pit in 1995.

The play deals with the problems of young love and adults' inabil-
ity to talk openly with their children. The story revolves around
Wendla and Moritz, who pay with their lives for the moral dishon-
esty of their parents. Moritz has failed to obtain a place in the Upper
Class at school, despite long hours of hard study. Unable to face his
parents' reaction to the news he makes up his mind to kill himself.

In this scene he is walking along a winding path at dusk through
marshy undergrowth. ILSE enters. Moritz is startled and accuses her
of sneaking up on him. She begins to talk about their schooldays
together, reminding him of how they used to play robbers and then
go back to her home in the evening for fresh goats milk. She remarks
that Moritz looks 'hungover' and he tells her that he has been up all
the previous night drinking. She is now working as an artist's model
and goes on to recount her adventures and narrow escapes at last
year's Carnival.

Published by Faber & Faber, London

ILSE

I don't know what a hangover is. Last carnival I never got to bed or changed my clothes for three days and three nights. From the ball to the café, the Bellavista at midday, cabaret in the evening, then back to the ball. Lena was there, and Viola – remember the fat girl? Then on the third night Heinrich found me. . . . He tripped over my arm. I was flat out unconscious in the snow on the street. He took me back to his place. I was there two weeks – what a ghastly fortnight that was! Mornings I had to swan about his apartment in his Persian bathrobe. Evenings it was his little black pageboy outfit. White lace at the throat, the wrists and the knees. Every day he'd photograph me in some exotic pose – Ariadne draped over the back of a sofa, or as Leda or Ganymede. Once down on all fours as a female Nebuchadnezzar. All the time he was ranting on about killing, shooting, suicide, gas. Then he'd jump up at three a.m. and come back to bed with a pistol, load it and stick it into my breast. 'Blink once,' he'd say, 'and I'll blast you wide open.' . . . Directly over his bed, in the ceiling, was a mirror. It made his tiny den seem to go straight up – like a tower, and very bright, like an opera house. You saw yourself hanging there in the heavens, face downwards. Every night I had the most horrible nightmares. Then I would lie awake just gritting my teeth to make the hours pass – please God, make it morning soon. Good night, Ilse. When you are asleep, do you know, my darling, you are beautiful enough to murder. . . . I pray to God he's dead. One day while he was out for his absinthe, I slipped his coat on and got away down the street. Carnival time was long past and the police picked me up. So it's what am I doing in a man's coat and straight off to the police station. Then in came Nohl, Fehrendorf, Padinsky, Spuhler, Oikonomopulos, the whole Phallopia, and they bailed me out. They took me off to Adolar's in a cab. So ever since I've stuck with them. Fehrendorf is a baboon. Nohl is an arsehole. Bojokewitsch is a blockhead. Boison has no principles whatever. And Oikonomopulos is a clown. But I love them all and wouldn't hook up with anybody else, even if the rest of the world were nothing but angels and billionaires.

TINA
America
45-ish

THE STRIP
Phyllis Nagy

First performed at the Royal Court Theatre in 1995, it follows the fortunes of Ava Coo, a female impersonator, a love-struck repossession man and an obsessive lesbian journalist, as they cross America in search of fame and self gratification at the Luxor Hotel, Las Vegas. Meanwhile, in Earls Court, an astrologer, a family of white supremacists and a gay pawnbroker set off to Liverpool in search of justice. Moving amongst them all is the mysterious Otto Mink.

In this scene, set in the Ladies room of the 'Tumbleweed Junction', Las Vagas, Ava Coo's mother, TINA is on her hands and knees scrubbing the floor. She has a scrubbing brush in one hand and a small dictaphone, belonging to her employer, Mr Greene (alias Otto Mink) in the other. She is recording a message for Ava.

Published by Methuen Publishing, London

TINA

Dear Ava. I probably didn't get your last letter because when I married Mr. Marshall, I moved house. Not that my split level wasn't nice enough for us but . . . well now I live on a one-hundred and fifty acre ranch with Mr. Marshall. And before that, I was so busy at the casino I was hardly ever home to get my mail. But I know you wrote to me, Ava. And I know what you wrote about because let's face it honey, all our letters say the same thing. The weather is good, the weather is bad, and so on. I put pen to paper and I find myself writing the same old things, who knows why. So I am sending you a tape in the hope that it will change our routine. Mr. Marshall gave me this Dictaphone as a wedding gift and you know I've always been a freer talker than a writer. You would like Mr. Marshall. He's tall and rarely speaks. But he opens doors for me and buys me bunches of daisies from the Seven-Eleven and really, Ava, that's more than good enough. I miss your voice, honey. It's hard being a casino supervisor in Vegas, but it's rewarding. As you can imagine, I don't make many friends on the gaming floor, but I am a fair boss and last week I got Dolly Parton's autograph. Mr. Marshall breeds horses. I keep an eye out for promising colts. So far there's no hint of a Secretariat, but his horses are strong and good looking. Like him. I am babbling and so I better get to the point of this letter which is: I think I saw your daddy's picture in a newspaper last week. I say I think it was him because I haven't seen him in twenty years but it looked just like him. Except in the newspapers his name was Marquette and he looked much thinner than when I knew him. I think he killed twenty-seven people at a truck stop in Lynchburg. Well. That's all for now. I hope you are still enjoying success as a cabaret singer. I am so proud of you, Ava. With love, your mother, Mrs. Tina Coo Marshall.

(Otto *enters*.)

You're not supposed to be in here, Mr. Greene. This is the ladies room. . . . We're, uhm, running out of extra strength Lysol. . . . I had to bring some from home today. Will we be getting it on delivery any time soon? . . . I can't clean the toilets without it.

OLGA
35

SUMMERFOLK
Maxim Gorky
A new version by Nick Dear

This version was first performed in the Olivier auditorium of the Royal National Theatre in 1999.

In the early years of the twentieth century, Russians of every social class were beginning to sense the onset of a great upheaval. A diverse group of Russians meet, as they do every year, at their Summer holiday retreat. Some are frightened at the prospect of change, some are angry and some yearn for a new life. As they question the value of their work, their art and their leisure, relationships break under the strain and scandals of business and infidelity are laid bare. OLGA is married to Kiril Dudakov, the doctor in charge of the local hospital. Forever moaning, she is nevertheless driven to distraction by her screaming children and their new nanny.

It is early evening. In this scene OLGA strolls along the path towards her friend, Varvara's dacha. Varvara comes out onto the terrace to meet her. Almost immediately OLGA starts complaining about her husband 'running away from family life'. Prone to exaggeration, she works herself into a frenzy, finally insulting Varvara, who announces she is leaving.

(A 'dacha' is a Russian country cottage used especially in summer.)

Published by Faber & Faber, London

OLGA *(Quietly.)*

Well. Have you any idea why he's like that? . . . He dashes back from town, spends two minutes with the children, then dashes out again! Hardly guaranteed to make me leap for joy, is it?

(They wander towards the trees.)

. . . He's running away from family life, that's what he's doing. I know, I know, he's overworked, he needs a break, but what about me? Don't I get a break? I work myself into the ground! And nothing I can do or say is right. Lord! It makes me livid! He needs reminding that I've sacrificed my youth, my looks, everything – all for him! . . . I feel I should say to him: 'I'm going away! Taking the children and going away!' . . . I owe you too much already! . . . I hate myself for not being able to manage without your help. Do you think I like taking your husband's money? How can one have any self-respect, if one can't manage the household finances . . . can't get by without hand-outs? Well? Well? Do you know there are times when I don't like you? Loathe you in fact. Can't bear you. Always so calm and rational. Never showing any real *passion*! . . . I believe that those who are always helping others must, at the bottom of their hearts, despise the ones they're helping. Yes. And I'd like to be one of the helpers. . . . I don't like people! Why should I like people? I don't like Maria Lvovna – who does she think she is, to judge us from on high? . . . And Kaleria – arrogant hussy. Claims to be searching for truth and beauty – really looking for a man to take her to bed! . . . *(Softly, but maliciously.)* I do not care. I do not care where we go, as long as it's away from here, this unendurable drudgery! I want to live! I'm no worse than anyone else! I've got eyes in my head, I'm not thick! I can see that even you – oh, you live very nicely thank you, your husband's made some money – not a hundred per cent honestly, either, according to what people say – you've contrived – somehow – not to tie yourself down with screaming children! . . .

(Varvara *stands and stares at* OLGA, *completely amazed.*)

Varya, I didn't mean it . . . Don't look at me like that . . . I'm only repeating what everyone knows about your husband . . . . . . I've said something awful, haven't I? Please, please forgive me. I'm so nasty!

VARVARA
27

SUMMERFOLK
Maxim Gorky
A new version by Nick Dear

This version was first performed in the Olivier auditorium of the Royal National Theatre in 1999.

In the early years of the twentieth century, Russians of every social class were beginning to sense the onset of a great upheaval. A diverse group of Russians meet, as they do every year, at their Summer holiday retreat. Some are frightened at the prospect of change, some are angry and some yearn for a new life. As they question the value of their work, their art and their leisure, relationships break under the strain and scandals of business and infidelity are laid bare.

In this scene it is late afternoon at the end of a picnic. The men are telling jokes and the musicians are playing in the background. Everyone has had a few drinks. VARVARA is the wife of the lawyer, Sergei Bassov. She is dissatisfied both with her life and her marriage. She sits with her friends Kaleria and Yulia on bales of straw in a clearing in the woods, listening to the music. For VARVARA it brings back memories.

Published by Faber & Faber, London

VARVARA

Reminds me of a song the washerwomen used to sing, in the place where my mother worked. I think I'd just started school. I remember the laundry full of grey steam, and half-dressed women, singing in tired voices:

Mother, pity me
Your poor little girl
Crying among strangers
Alone in the world.

Used to make me weep, that song. . . . I had a good life then . . . ! Those rough women loved me. When they'd finished work in the evenings, they used to drink tea at a long, scrubbed pine table – and they'd sit me down among them, as if I was grown-up, too. . . . My mother slaved for forty years, yet you can't conceive how generous she was! And how cheerful! Everybody adored her. She pushed me to study – I remember her utter joy when I graduated from college. She could barely walk by that time. Rheumatism. And when she died she said, 'Don't cry, Varya. It's nothing. You live, you work, and then it's time to go.' I think there was a lot more meaning to her life than there is to mine. I feel clumsy and ignorant, a stranger in a strange land, out of my depth. I don't understand the world in which cultured people live. It seems so brittle, knocked together fast like booths at the fair. No, like ice fragments floating on a river . . . they gleam and glitter, but they're riddled with dirt, with shame . . . Whenever I read a really honest, straightforward book, a courageous book, it's as if the sun is rising, a light of truth in the sky, and it will melt the filthy ice, and the pure, clean water will wash it away . . .

POLYXENA
young

TANTALUS
John Barton

First performed at the Denver Center for the Performing Arts in October 2000 and transferred to the Barbican Theatre, London in May 2001 after a short tour. *Tantalus* is the epic tale of the Trojan War, described as 'a crusade which became a catastrophe'. It is divided into three parts, *The Outbreak of War*, *The War*, and *The Homecoming*, and is made up of ten plays, one of which is *Odysseus*.

In this play Troy has been overthrown and King Priam slain. Queen Hecuba and the Trojan Women have been taken captive. At the opening scene they are all sitting or lying around the fire as Odysseus enters with his soldiers bearing food. He treats them kindly, commiserating on the death of their king and the burning and looting of Troy, which he excuses as an unavoidable 'mistake'. He explains that they have, as is the custom, been chosen, as 'war prizes'. He himself has chosen Hecuba - not for his bed - but to protect her as she once saved his life. Neoptolemus, the slayer of Priam will have two 'prizes', one for himself and one for his dead father, Achilles. This second choice has fallen on Hecuba's daughter, POLYXENA. Hecuba protests wildly, but Odysseus replies that he has no say in the matter. POLYXENA tells her mother to be quiet. She knows that to be the prize of a dead man means human sacrifice and explains why she is prepared to die.

Published by Oberon Books, London

POLYXENA
You must stop this, mother;
Be quiet and listen to me.
After Achilles died
Cassandra told me what would happen
But I shut it out of my mind
As you are trying to do now.

Quiet, Mother. You have spoken
Fine words about the future
Because it's against the rules
For those who govern kingdoms
To dare to speak the truth.
You left out the one word that matters:
We are slaves. Each one of you
Will scrub floors and be whipped
If you do not please your masters;
You will sweat all day in the fields
And at night share some brute's bed
And his snores will mock your memories.
I would rather die than be chosen
For the bed of the butcher-boy
Who killed my dear father.

Take me to my husband
And let Calchas cut my throat;
I want that, yes, I want it:
It is said that all dead men
Love to drink the blood of the living
Because it gives them the sense
Of being alive again.
Achilles does not call for me
Because he wants revenge
But because he loves his wife.
If there had been time
For us to be together
As a man and wife should be
We would have made peace
Between Troy and the West
And I would have learned to love him.
If my blood now can give him
A little sense of life
I shall be a true wife to him. . . .
I shall see my father
Underneath the earth
And meet all my brothers
And Hector will hug me
As he did when I was little.
Why should I fear Asphodel
When at last I will be able
To tell Paris what I think of him?

SANDIE
mid 30s

TOPLESS
Miles Tredinnick

This one-woman play was first presented in London by Open Top Productions in association with the Big Bus Company in 1999 and is set on the open top of a London sightseeing bus on a summer's day.

SANDIE is a tour guide on a 'fabulous' tour of London on an open top sightseeing bus. She can't wait to point out all the sights from Big Ben to the Tower of London and explain their history. Unfortunately that's not all she wants to talk about. Domestic problems and sightseeing become intertwined as she reveals how she deals with her straying husband.

In this opening scene she is reading from a clip-board in dreadful French. Nobody is listening to her and she realises something is wrong. The group she is talking to are not from Calais after all.

Published by Comedy Hall Books, London

SANDIE
Bienvenue a Londres et Bienvenue chez 'London Topless Buses'. Le 'Topless' est le moyen idéal de visiter sans effort les sites touristiques de Londres. Je m'appelle Sandie et notre chauffeur est Sid . . . . *(She realises something is wrong and shouts down the stairwell.)* Sid? Are you sure this is the group from Calais? Because they don't seem particularly French to me. They've what? Cancelled? Oh. Well thanks for telling me. *(Facing audience.)* So you all speak English do you? Well I won't be needing that. *(She puts the clip-board down on one of the front seats.)* Hi everyone and welcome to London. My name's Sandie and I'm your tour guide. How are you all? Everyone OK? I'm feeling absolutely brilliant today. I am. Honestly. Now I know what you're thinking. The wheel's turning but the hamster's dead. But don't worry, I haven't got going yet. I'm building up to my tour de force and believe me it'll be worth waiting for. We're going to

have a fabulous tour. Now 'cos I thought you were all going to be foreign I've brought along a few *visual aids* to jazz things up a bit. *(She opens her bag and hands out various London souvenirs starting with a miniature Big Ben.)* This is Big Ben which we'll be seeing later. Who wants Big Ben? *(She then takes out a little Beefeater doll.)* And here's one of the Yeoman Warders you'll see down the Tower. *(Next she produces a policeman's helmet and puts it on a man's head.)* Evening all! *(She salutes him.)* Love your helmet sir. Smashing. *(She holds up a large plastic cigar.)* And what's this one? It's Winston Churchill, ain't it. *(She hands it to someone.)* You hold that and wave it when I get to me Churchill bit. *(She then holds up something wrapped in silver foil.)* And what have we got 'ere? Oh me sandwiches. Only cheese and tomato I'm afraid. If anyone wants to do a swop later I'm game. Provided it's not meat. I'm a veggie. Right, that's the basics dealt with so off we go. *(She presses the bus bell button twice.)* Now our driver is called Sid, he's the best driver in the country. Hopeless in town but in the country he's brilliant!

(The bus starts up. It jerks off. SANDIE grabs a safety rail to steady herself.)

See what I mean!! Hold on tight! Right, now I'm going to take you on a fabulous trip around London. I'm going to show you all the big sights. Trafalgar Square, Big Ben, Westminster Abbey, St Paul's Cathedral, all the way down to the Tower of London. So sit back and enjoy yourselves. If you've got any questions keep them to yourselves! I haven't got time for questions, I'll be too busy talking! I'm the original motormouth, me.

(She turns to take in the first sight.)

Right, now we're kicking off in Piccadilly.

VERONICA
South African
17

VALLEY SONG
Athol Fugard

First performed at the Royal Court Theatre Downstairs in January 1996. This play is about the fears, hopes and dreams of the people in a new South Africa, and is set in a small village in the Sneuberg Mountains.

Old Buks, ex-corporal in the famous Coloured regiment, the Cape Corps, worries about the Whiteman buying the old Landman house and taking over his piece of land – his 'akkers'. His granddaughter, VERONICA, dreams of eventually leaving the village and going to Johannesburg to study singing.

In this scene VERONICA is talking to the audience. Her mood is dark and defiant.

('Oupa' = grandfather; 'Ouma' = grandmother.)

Published by Faber & Faber, London

VERONICA *(To the audience. Her mood is dark and defiant.)*
I hate those akkers. Yes. Hate them. I know that's a big sin - to hate
the Earth what God created - but I can't help it. That's the way I feel
and that's what I want to say. If I was my Oupa I would rather let us
go hungry than plant another seed in that ground. I mean it.
It gives us food, but it takes our lives. Oh yes, it does! That's why my
mother ran away. I just know it. She didn't want her life to be buried
in that old house the way my Ouma's was. If ever anybody sees a
spook in that house it will be my Ouma . . . scrubbing the floors.
And my Oupa also . . . he'll spook those akkers one day. You'll see.
He's like a slave now to that little piece of land. That's all he lives for,
and it's not even his. He talks about nothing else, worries about
nothing else, prays for nothing else . . . 'Come, Veronica, let us hold
hands and pray for rain.' 'Come, Veronica, let us hold hands and pray
that there is no late frost.' 'Come, Veronica, let us hold hands and
pray that the bees don't sting the young pumpkins.'
Well, what about me? I'm also a living thing you know. I also want
to grow. What about: Come, everybody, let us hold hands and pray
that the bees don't sting the young Veronica.

EDIE
Warwickshire/Coventry
40s

A WARWICKSHIRE TESTIMONY
April De Angelis

First performed by the Royal Shakespeare Company at The Other Place, Stratford-Upon-Avon in 1999. The play takes place in a small Warwickshire village and is written around the 'testimonies' of members of local communities who were invited to contribute memories and impressions of past and present experiences. We see the past, with the 'big house', the servant class, and the close-knit family ties of a bygone generation, and the present with its eye to big business, where nothing stays the same for long and the 'quaint-ness' of the cottages is all that's left of village life.

Desperate to get away from the family and a culture where every-body knows everything about everybody, EDIE leaves home. Throughout the action we see fragments of her life – sometimes as a young girl, then again as a grown woman after the war with her own hairdressing business, and as an eighty-two year old woman in an old people's home.

The scene is set in EDIE's hairdressing salon in 1962. George, who was married to her sister, Margery, has just finished laying a bit of carpet at the entrance. EDIE sends her assistant off home and offers George a drink. He is anxious to get away, but she persuades him to stay for a while.

Published by Faber & Faber, London

EDIE

Now. George. You are not going anywhere till you have a drink. . . .
Well, stay with me while I have one, George. Stop lurking by the door.
Sit down.

(He sits. She gets herself a drink.)

. . . You must miss Margery. . . . I miss her too.

I like working for myself. I've saved quite a bit. . . . But somehow I
feel I'm missing something. . . . I've had some scrapes.

(She gets out a magazine. Shows it to George.*)*

(She reads aloud.) True Life Crimes. . . . page 17. I went out with him
for a bit. *(She points to picture.)* . . . *(Reads.)* 'Tall, handsome, young
airforce -' . . . Well, he was dressed as airforce. . . . *(Reads.)* 'Neville
Church was a suave sex maniac, one of the most violently depraved
men the world has ever known. On a few summer days he haunted
England's genteel South Coast.' . . . He done a chain murder down in
Brighton. I knew him for about six weeks. One night I was waiting up
St Nicholas Church street for Neville and up come Bernie with her
boyfriend. 'Where's Neville,' I says. Bernie's boyfriend got out the car,
he says 'Edie, you'll never see him again.' I said, 'Never? Why?' He put
his hands on my shoulders, he says, 'Consider yourself a very lucky
girl.' And the next fortnight after that he done a chain murder. Then
one day he pulled up at the Coventry traffic lights and he says, 'What
you looking at, Edie?' I says, 'Your eyes, I've never seen eyes like them'.
They were red and blue and white and purple. Do you know what
happened? It's perfectly true. He went to kiss me and I belched and
he just pushed my head to one side like he used to do before he
murdered them and he said, 'Urgh, Edie, what you been eating?'
'Pilchards on toast,' I said, 'I love 'em.' He couldn't get rid of me quick
enough. I'm sure that's what saved my life. . . . That's why I'm looking
for someone normal. Someone I can trust.

(Pause.)

I didn't really need a new bit of carpet. I mean it's lovely and all that.
I just wanted to see you. You always promised you'd pop round but
you never did. Aren't you lonely, George? . . . You like a pair of arms
around you, don't you? Everybody does. You know everything about
me, George. All my secrets. It's as if you were there at all the right
times. That means something. You've always liked me a bit haven't
you? . . . We could be much happier together than on our own. . . .
You can come and live here, over the shop. And in a way it's fair.
Margery had half of you and now I can have the other half.

OLD EDIE
Warwickshire/Coventry
82

A WARWICKSHIRE TESTIMONY
April De Angelis

First performed by the Royal Shakespeare Company at The Other Place, Stratford-Upon-Avon in 1999. The play takes place in a small Warwickshire village and is written around the 'testimonies' of members of local communities who were invited to contribute memories and impressions of past and present experiences. We see the past, with the 'big house', the servant class, and the close-knit family ties of a bygone generation, and the present with its eye to big business, where nothing stays the same for long and the 'quaintness' of the cottages is all that's left of village life.

Desperate to get away from the family and a culture where everybody knows everything about everybody else, EDIE leaves home. Throughout the action we see fragments of her life – sometimes as a young girl, then again as a grown woman after the war with her own hairdressing business, and as an eighty-two year old woman in an old people's home.

In this scene OLD EDIE is back in the cottage she left as a young girl. The cottage is now occupied by her niece, Dorothy and husband, Tom, who she has persuaded to bring her out of the home before she 'turns soft'. EDIE is alone. It is early morning and still dark.

Published by Faber & Faber, London

EDIE

Blinkin' hell.

What've you done, Edie Cox? How come you're back here? Why spend a lifetime avoiding a place and then end up stuck there in your twilight years? Poor Dorothy. She's not right, is she? She's been through it – losing that child. And living in a village doesn't help. Her nose stuck in the past. Why don't you tell her the truth? People may look all angelic and innocent and fuzzy in those old photos but they could be bastards all the same. Just like now. You've taken advantage of Dorothy, you have. You're a wicked old woman and what are you going to do about it? You're no good to anyone. Worse. You're trouble. Dorothy's a good niece. She always brought you your favourite biscuits an' all. Hobnobs, and they're not cheap. This place brings out the worst in you. It hasn't changed. Same doors, same floor. I can see you, Mum, sewing something in the corner. Shrouds probably. That was what you used to make. Four for two bob. And there's Margery drying her stockings in front of the fire. I don't like meeting you all again I can tell you. I can feel you in the shadows waiting to step out. Well, that's not how it's going to be. You can stick to the damp and the corners. I'm shutting me mouth from now on. If I was young I'd leave. Pack me case. Sneak out early one morning when the air is still and the sun just creeping up. Grip the handle of my suitcase. My young feet are quick. Trip trip they go. And then I'm away, free. Best thing I ever did. That was when my life started. Me real life.

VALERIE
Irish/Dublin
30s

THE WEIR
Conor McPherson

First performed at the Royal Court Theatre Upstairs in 1997 and then at the Duke of York's Theatre, London in 1998.

The action takes place in present time in a bar in a rural part of Ireland – Northwest Leitrim or Sligo. Barman, Brendan, and locals Finbar, Jack and Jim, are swapping ghost stories to impress VALERIE, a young woman from Dublin newly moved into the area. One of these stories concerning a child obviously disturbs her and she asks the way to the Ladies' cloakroom. When she returns Finbar announces that they've had enough of the stories. There must be no more of them. VALERIE insists that she'd like to tell them something that happened to her personally, concerning her five-year old daughter who had died the previous year in an accident in the swimming pool at the Central Remedial Clinic.

Published by Nick Hern Books, London

VALERIE

But, and then one morning. I was in bed, Daniel had gone to work. I usually lay there for a few hours, trying to stay asleep, really. I suppose. And the phone rang. And I just left it. I wasn't going to get it. And it rang for a long time. Em, eventually it stopped and I was dropping off again. But then it started ringing again, for a long time. So I thought it must have been Daniel trying to get me. Someone who knew I was there.

So I went down and answered it. And. The line was very faint. It was like a crossed line. There were voices, but I couldn't hear what they were saying. And then I heard Niamh. She said, 'Mammy?' And I . . . just said, you know, 'Yes.'

(Short pause.)

And she said . . . She wanted me to come and collect her. I mean, I wasn't sure whether this was a dream or her leaving us had been a dream. I just said, 'Where are you?'

And she said she thought she was at Nana's. In the bedroom. But Nana wasn't there. And she was scared. There were children knocking in the walls and the man was standing across the road, and he was looking up and he was going to cross the road. And would I come and get her?

And I said I would, of course I would. And I dropped the phone and I ran out to the car in just a teeshirt I slept in. And I drove to Daniel's mother's house. And I could hardly see. I was crying so much. I mean. I knew she wasn't going to be there. I knew she was gone. But to think wherever she was . . . that . . . And there was nothing I could do about it.

Daniel's mother got a doctor and I . . . slept for a day or two. But it was . . . Daniel felt that I . . . needed to face up to Niamh being gone. But I just thought that he should face up to what happened to me. He was insisting I get some treatment, and then . . . everything would be okay. But you know, what can help that, if she's out there? She still . . . she still needs me.

(Pause.)

An excerpt (abridged) from *The Weir* by Conor McPherson.
Published by Nick Hern Books, The Glasshouse,
49a Goldhawk Road, London W12 8QP.

USEFUL ADDRESSES

The Academy Drama School,
189 Whitechapel Road,
London, E1 1DN
Tel: 020 7377 8735

The Actors' Theatre School,
32 Exeter Road
London, NW2 4SB
Tel: 020 8450 0371

Penny Dyer
Dialect Coach
Tel: 020 8543 2946

Barry Grantham
806 Howard House
Dolphin Square
London SW1V 3PQ
Tel: 020 7798 8246

The Guildhall School of Music and Drama,
Barbican,
London, EC2Y 8DT
Tel: 020 7628 2571

London Academy of Music and Dramatic Art (LAMDA)
Tower House,
226 Cromwell Road,
London, SW5 0SR
Tel: 020 7373 9883

Offstage Theatre and Film Bookshop,
37 Chalk Farm Road,
London, NW1 8AJ
Tel: 020 7485 4996

Royal Academy of Dramatic Art,
62/64 Gower Street,
London, WC1E 6ED
Tel: 020 7636 7076

Spotlight, (*Casting Directory* and *Contacts*)
7 Leicester Place,
London, WC2H 7BP
Tel: 020 7437 7631

COPYRIGHT HOLDERS

Edited extract from *The Absence of War* by David Hare. Reproduced by permission of Faber & Faber Ltd. Published by Faber & Faber Ltd., London.

An excerpt (abridged) from *Albertine in Five Times* by Michel Tremblay, translated by John Van Burek, Bill Glassco. Published by Nick Hern Books, The Glasshouse, 49a Goldhawk Road, London W12 8QP.

Edited extract from *Battle Royal* by Nick Stafford. Reproduced by permission of Faber & Faber Ltd. Published by Faber & Faber Ltd., London.

An excerpt (abridged) from *Bold Girls* by Rona Munro. Published by Hodder & Stoughton, London. Reproduced by permission of Nick Hern Books, The Glasshouse, 49a Goldhawk Road, London W12 8QP.

Excerpts (abridged) from *The Clink* by Stephen Jeffreys. Published by Nick Hern Books, The Glasshouse, 49a Goldhawk Road, London W12 8QP.

Extract from *The Colour of Justice*, edited by Richard Norton-Taylor. Based on the transcripts of the Stephen Lawrence Inquiry. Reproduced by permission of Oberon Books Ltd. Published by Oberon Books, London.

Excerpts from *Comic Potential* by Alan Ayckbourn. Copyright © 1999 by Alan Ayckbourn. Reprinted by permission of Faber and Faber, Inc., an affiliate of Farrar, Straus and Giroux, LLC and Faber & Faber Ltd. Published by Faber & Faber Ltd., London.

Extract from *Easter* by August Strindberg, translated by Peter Watts. Taken from *Three Plays by August Strindberg*. Copyright © Peter Watts, 1958. Reproduced by permission of Penguin Books Ltd. Published by Penguin Classics, London (1958).

Extract from *The Editing Process* by Meredith Oakes. Reproduced by permission of Oberon Books Ltd. Published by Oberon Books, London.

Excerpts (abridged) from *The Guid Sisters* by Michel Tremblay. Translated by Bill Findlay and Martin Bowman. Published by Nick Hern Books, The Glasshouse, 49a Goldhawk Road, London W12 8QP.

Extract from *Harvest* by Ellen Dryden. Reproduced by permission of First Writes Publications. Published in 1996 by First Writes Publications, London in *Harvest and Other Plays*. Originally published by Samuel French. All rights whatsoever in this play are strictly reserved and application for performance etc. must be made before rehearsal to Casarotto Ramsay & Associates Ltd., National House, 60-66 Wardour Street, London W1V 4ND. No performance may be given unless a licence has been obtained. Applications for amateur performance must be made to Samuel French Ltd., 52 Fitzroy Street, London W1P 6JR.

Extract from *The Herbal Bed* © 1996 Peter Whelan. Reprinted by permission of Josef Weinberger Ltd., 12-14 Mortimer Street, London W1T 3JJ. Applications for amateur performance rights must be made to Josef Weinberger Ltd. All rights reserved.

Edited extract from *House and Garden* by Alan Ayckbourn. Reproduced by permission of Faber & Faber Ltd. Published by Faber & Faber Ltd., London.

Extract from *In the Sweat* by Naomi Wallace and Bruce McLeod. Taken from *New Connections - New Plays for Young People*. Reproduced by permission of The Rod Hall Agency Limited. Published by Faber & Faber Ltd., London

Extract from *Indian Summer* by Lucy Maurice. Copyright © Lucy Maurice. Reproduced by permission of First Writes Publications. Published in 1999 by First Writes Publications, Norfolk.

Extract from *A Jovial Crew* © 1992 Stephen Jeffreys. Reprinted by permission of Josef Weinberger Ltd., 12-14 Mortimer Street, London W1T 3JJ. Applications for amateur performance rights must be made to Josef Weinberger Ltd. All rights reserved.

An excerpt (abridged) from *Kindertransport* by Diane Samuels. Published by Nick Hern Books, The Glasshouse, 49a Goldhawk Road, London W12 8QP.

Edited extract from *The Lady in the Van* by Alan Bennett. Reprinted by permission of PFD on behalf of: Alan Bennett. © Alan Bennett: as printed in the original volume. Also reproduced by permission of Faber & Faber Ltd. Published by Faber & Faber Ltd., London.

Edited extract from *Life is Sweet* by Mike Leigh. Reproduced by permission of Faber & Faber Ltd. Published by Faber & Faber Ltd., London.

Edited extract from *Madame Melville* by Richard Nelson. Copyright agent ML 2000 Ltd., Douglas House, 16-18 Douglas Street, London SW1P 4PB. Also reproduced by permission of Faber & Faber Ltd. Published by Faber & Faber Ltd., London.

An excerpt (abridged) from *Manon/Sandra* by Michel Tremblay, translated by John Van Burek. Published by Nick Hern Books, The Glasshouse, 49a Goldhawk Road, London W12 8QP.

The Member of the Wedding. Copyright © Floria V. Lasky, Executrix of the Estate of Carson McCullers. Published by New Directions, New York.

Edited extract from *Mules* by Winsome Pinnock. Reproduced by permission of Faber & Faber Ltd. Published by Faber & Faber Ltd., London.

Edited extract from *Murmuring Judges* by David Hare. Reproduced by permission of Faber & Faber Ltd. Published by Faber & Faber Ltd., London.

Oroonoko © 'Biyi Bandele, reproduced by permission of Amber

Lane Press Ltd. Published by Amber Lane Press, Charlbury, Oxfordshire.

An excerpt (abridged) from *Pentecost* by David Edgar. Published by Nick Hern Books, The Glasshouse, 49a Goldhawk Road, London W12 8QP.

An excerpt (abridged) from *Perfect Days* by Liz Lochhart. Published by Nick Hern Books, The Glasshouse, 49a Goldhawk Road, London W12 8QP.

An excerpt (abridged) from *A Place at the Table* by Simon Block. Published by Nick Hern Books, The Glasshouse, 49a Goldhawk Road, London W12 8QP.

Edited extract from *Playhouse Creatures* by April De Angelis. Reproduced by permission of Faber & Faber Ltd. Published by Faber & Faber Ltd., London.

Extract from *Portia Coughlan* by Marina Carr. Reproduced by permission of The Agency (London) Ltd. © Marina Carr. Published by Faber & Faber Ltd., London.

Edited extract from *The Positive Hour* by April De Angelis. Reproduced by permission of Faber & Faber Ltd. Published by Faber & Faber Ltd., London.

Extracts from *The Power of the Dog* by Ellen Dryden. Reproduced by permission of First Writes Publications. Published in 1996 by First Writes Publications, London. All rights whatsoever in this play are strictly reserved and application for performance etc. must be made before rehearsal to Casarotto Ramsay & Associates Ltd., National House, 60-66 Wardour Street, London W1V 4ND. No performance may be given unless a licence has been obtained. Applications for amateur performance must be made to Samuel French Ltd., 52 Fitzroy Street, London W1P 6JR.

Extract from *A Prayer for Wings* © Sean Mathias, reproduced by permission of Amber Lane Press Ltd. Published by Amber Lane Press, Charlbury, Oxfordshire.

Extract from *Pride and Prejudice* stage adaptation by Sue Pomeroy. Reprinted by permission of Sue Pomeroy.

From *Pulp Fiction: A Quentin Tarantino Screenplay*. Copyright © 1994 Quentin Tarantino. Reprinted by permission of Hyperion. Also reproduced by permision of Faber & Faber Ltd. Published by Faber & Faber Ltd., London.

The Rainmaker by N. Richard Nash. Copyright © by N. Richard Nash. Reprinted by permission of William Morris Agency, Inc. on behalf of the Author.

Edited extract from *Spring Awakening* by Frank Wedekind. A new version by Ted Hughes. Reproduced by permission of Faber & Faber Ltd. Published by Faber & Faber Ltd., London.

Edited extract from *The Strip* by Phyllis Nagy. Reproduced by permission of Methuen Publishing Ltd. Published by Methuen Publishing Ltd., London.

Edited extracts from *Summerfolk* by Maxim Gorky. A new version by Nick Dear. Reproduced by permision of Faber & Faber Ltd. Published by Faber & Faber Ltd., London.

Extract from *Tantalus* by John Barton. Reproduced by permission of Oberon Books Ltd. Published by Oberon Books, London.

Extract from *Topless* by Miles Tredinnick. Reproduced by permission of Comedy Hall Books, 26 Vermeer Court, Rembrandt Close, London E14 3XA.

Extract from *Valley Song* by Athol Fugard. Copyright © 1996 by Athol Fugard. Reprinted by permission of William Morris Agency, Inc. on behalf of the Author. Also reproduced by permission of Faber & Faber Ltd. Published by Faber & Faber Ltd., London.

Edited extracts from *A Warwickshire Testimony* by April De Angelis. Reproduced by permission of Faber & Faber Ltd. Published by Faber & Faber Ltd., London.

An excerpt (abridged) from *The Weir* by Conor McPherson. Published by Nick Hern Books, The Glasshouse, 49a Goldhawk Road, London W12 8QP.

Every effort has been made to trace and acknowledge copyright owners. If any right has been omitted the publishers offer their apologies and will rectify this in subsequent editions following notification.